GREEN AND PLEASANT LAND
A Countryman Remembers

GREEN AND PLEASANT LAND

A Countryman Remembers

NORMAN MURSELL

Illustrated by Rodger McPhail

London
GEORGE ALLEN & UNWIN
Boston   Sydney

DEDICATED TO

my wife, Eileen, and children, Malcolm and
Jeanette, for all their encouragement and help;

the Duke of Westminster and the Grosvenor
family, for whom I worked for fifty happy
years;

and not least all my friends past and present,
without whom this book would not be
possible.

Text © Norman Mursell, 1983
Illustrations © Rodger McPhail, 1983

George Allen & Unwin (Publishers) Ltd,
40 Museum Street, London WC1A 1LU, UK

George Allen & Unwin (Publishers) Ltd,
Park Lane, Hemel Hempstead, Herts HP2 4TE, UK

Allen & Unwin Inc.,
9 Winchester Terrace, Winchester, Mass 01890, USA

George Allen & Unwin Australia Pty Ltd,
8 Napier Street, North Sydney, NSW 2060, Australia

First published in 1983

British Library Cataloguing in Publication Data

Mursell, Norman
  Green and pleasant land.
1. Country life—Cheshire   2. Natural history
—Cheshire
I. Title
942.7'1'0924   S522.G7
ISBN 0-04-799015-5

Set in 12 on 13 point Caslon
by Alan Sutton Publishing Limited, Gloucester
and printed in Great Britain by
Mackays of Chatham

FOREWORD

by His Grace the Duke of Westminster

The time span which this book covers has seen many changes in our countryside and the way of life that goes with it, some for the better and some for the worse. But we must never forget that the countryside, with all its connotations, never stops changing, particularly as it has done since the repeal of the Corn Laws, through the Industrial Revolution and two World Wars.

Its way of life has had to adapt to the changing fortunes of time, for the countryside is made up of two important elements: the diversity of the landscape and the diversity of the people who live and work in it; and the people remembered within these pages help to make rural life the rich pattern that it is. It is for this reason, and indeed many others, that we owe them a great debt of gratitude. I have no hesitation in commending this book to you.

1

The lone ploughman, with his single-furrow, horse-drawn plough, plodding the land for long hours, was a symbol of pre-war farming. Today he is quite vanished – just one of the many changes in our countryside in the last half-century. Although the rural areas have seen less dramatic changes, by and large, than the cities, in many cases the transformation has been extreme. This is a story of rural Cheshire over the last fifty years, recording some of the changes, some of the activities and some of the characters, mainly on a large estate just south of Chester: the Eaton Estate, owned for centuries by the Grosvenor family.

This estate of about twelve thousand acres is still maintained to a very high standard as most estates go, and like the majority of Cheshire is mainly dairy farming. In the early 'thirties a large number of people worked on the estate and every farm had several hands, the home farm at one time employing thirty-two men. The forestry department had in

1

the region of seventy employees, the gardens at the Hall needed thirty-four gardeners to maintain them, there were twenty gamekeepers, a large staff in the clerk of works' department and seven or eight men on the stud farm where racehorses were bred. Then of course there was the staff at the Hall itself, from the second Duke of Westminster's personal and private secretary, the clerk to the household, down to the humble chambermaid and odd-job man. There were chefs, kitchen maids, parlour maids and footmen, a butler, two valets, three chauffeurs, and a housekeeper. On the permanent staff at the Hall were also a cabinet-maker, a plumber, an electrician and a night watchman, grooms to look after the horses and a number of employees to maintain the private golf course, not forgetting those who worked in the laundry. There must have been in the region of two hundred, nay, probably more, employed directly by the second Duke of Westminster and these were all controlled from the estate office charge of Major Basil Kerr with a staff of three or four!

When work ceased at night it was almost like workers going home from a modern-day factory, with man after man wending his way homeward along whichever drive led him to the village where he lived, maybe as much as three miles from the Hall. Some were on foot, some on cycles, but all of them were tired after a long day's labour which had begun at six-thirty in the morning and finished at five at night. Many of those employees had milked a cow and fed the pig and the hens before going to work, and would have more jobs facing them after their evening meal. What would the attitude of today's worker be to that?

But those employees were by and large a contented race. Many of them had followed in their fathers' footsteps and exercised great skills at their jobs, having had all the experience of many years handed down to them. Tough and hardy men, many of them lived to a good old age and worked until age or disability overtook them. With few exceptions they were a cheerful lot of men and gave rise to the inevitable characters: "Watty" Huxley, "Ham" Mellor, Jack Thomas, Tom ("The Cornerstone") Broster, and many others who will appear in future pages of this book.

2

These characters were always at their best at local events when, with radio (wireless, it was called then) only just started and television not invented, the only entertainment available had to be created by the villagers themselves. This applied throughout all rural areas, and at certain times of the year quite long journeys would be undertaken to support events taking place in other villages. There was a certain amount of rivalry between villages as to who could put on the best "do", but rarely was it anything other than friendly. More of these celebrations later.

The seasons – spring, summer, autumn, winter – seemed to be more defined in those days, and not just by the weather. Spring brought the working of the land and the sowing of the crops. Very little winter corn was sown before the war, so as March passed into April, every spare moment was spent cultivating the large cottage gardens and much interest was taken in the coming of spring – waiting and watching for the arrival of the swallow, listening for the first call of the cuckoo. Here friendly rivalry came into play. It was deemed an honour to have your name in the local paper with a report of the first swallow or cuckoo, and most country workers entered this game. Usually both swallows and cuckoos came from the south along the course of a brook which ran parallel

with the river Dee, so men working in this area were favourably placed to report the arrivals. "Watty" Huxley, forester, somehow contrived to be working in this area during the appropriate time in April, and over a period of years must have won on points with his numbers of reports in the local *Chronicle*. Mind you, Watty was particularly observant and a character to boot, which sometimes led his workmates to doubt the authenticity of his report!

Spring brought the countryside to life with much activity on the land and in the villages. With many small farms and smallholdings, and many more men working on the land, it was a time of urgency to get the seed sown, as well as preparing for the "turning out" of the milking stock. On Eaton Estate, tenant farmers were not allowed to have stock on the land from early October until May Day, except horses and sheep, so come the spring all fences and hedges had to be checked to ensure that when the cattle were turned out to grass, they would remain in the fields intended for them. The local hunt having been over the land during the winter, there were sometimes gaps in the hedges, broken rails, and occasionally a gate that would no longer shut satisfactorily.

By the first few days in May, all was ready for letting the cattle have the first taste of tender young grass, but this process had to be watched closely as too big a feed would "bloat" the cattle: just an hour or two to start with was enough. The cowmen looked forward to this day as it meant less work in the shippons (cowsheds) – and it was hard work. Wheeling many wheelbarrows full of muck out of the building into the midden morning and night was time-consuming, and of course there were always the cattle to be fed twice a day.

Summertime meant long hours in the hayfields, hoeing and thinning the various root crops and, as most cottages had large gardens, plenty to do at home when the labours on the farms were finished for the day. Many of the estate workers also had their own farming activities; a large number had  outbuildings and usually kept a cow to provide milk for their own use. Pigs were also numerous in the villages, and most houses had a pig-sty. In fact they still have, but they are no longer put to the original use – the health authorities wouldn't allow it anyway! Workers with cattle had to have the means of feeding them, and the estate provided these means by setting aside various fields for the use of villagers. In Aldford, the village in which I have lived for the last forty-five years, there were four fields totalling about eighty acres. The largest of these fields, the "ley field", was used for grazing the milking cows. It is a sight long gone from the countryside, the cows from various cottages turned out onto the lanes to wend their way to the grazing field. The families took it in turns to drive the cows to the ley field and to bring them back at the appropriate time for milking. What would the schoolchildren of today say about having to walk a mile or so to bring the cows in at five in the morning, and then repeating the process after school? It was a really rural sight to see maybe twenty cows ambling up the lane – no hurry in those days – and, as they came to their respective gates, turning in without any prompting by the child or children driving them.

The ley fields provided summer grazing for cottagers' cattle on many parts of the vast estate, but there was also the winter to be taken care of. To provide for this, two fields called the "town fields" were divided into acres and half-acres, each acre defined by a large sandstone at each corner. Some cottagers were entitled to one acre, some to an acre and a half, and one or two to two acres, depending on the accommodation for cattle available at the cottage or even the size of the worker's family. This land was used to grow various crops, as the tenant preferred. Some grew turnips and mangolds, some corn (nearly always oats), and there was a mixture of maybe four or five crops on most of the holdings so that it was possible to provide a varied diet for the milking cows during the long winter. Also, different types of crop took different lengths of time to germinate, so "scuffling" (the clearing of weeds) was spread over a longer period; later, when the seedlings needed thinning, the same applied. One trick the cottagers used was to sow a quantity of carrot seed with the turnips, thus eking out the winter vegetables grown at home. Turnips, although making a large amount of leaf growth, were not so dense as mangolds, which gave the carrots a better chance to grow.

There was much activity in these fields throughout the spring, summer and autumn, when the whole family was enrolled to help bring in the crops. Few of these people had horses or implements, so the goodwill of the smaller farmers was essential for ploughing and harvesting crops, but in those days there seemed to be much more of the help-one-another spirit about so in the end all the crops would be harvested. No combine harvesters then, not even a binder: the corn was cut with a reaper, a machine that cut the corn and laid it in swaths. This was an improvement on the days when it had to be cut by the laborious method of swinging a scythe, but the corn still had to be tied by hand and set up in stooks to harden the grain. The saying was that after the stooks had been set up the church bells had to ring over them thrice before they were ready to cart to the barn or stack.

The root crops also involved much back-breaking labour, although after the area given over to such crops, perhaps a quarter of an acre, had been ploughed and worked, there was usually a seed drill available to sow the seed. One old chap scorned the use of a plough and, with his family, dug all of his holding by hand! Once the seeds germinated the drills had to be scuffled to keep the weeds down – no selective weedkillers in those days!

Corn, meaning in those days oats, was usually grown by the people who had an acre and a half, a third of the holding being given over to the production of grain and of straw, a most useful commodity for bedding the cattle down during the winter months. Less labour overall was needed to grow corn, but good weather was essential at harvest time. Those men worked long hours and enjoyed no holidays, but had to rely on the summer and autumn evenings to get the crops harvested. A long wet spell at the wrong time could almost mean disaster for them, but the smaller local farmers, although hard-pressed themselves, would usually give a hand to retrieve the situation.

As well as these arable crops, hay had to be made, the mainstay of the winter feed. Meadow land was rented from Eaton Estate for this purpose – Radley Meadow, a large field of about fifty acres close to the river Dee. Like the town fields, this was divided into acres (no half-acres here), and

6

once again each area was marked by a large sandstone. Being by the river, the field was flooded practically every winter – in fact, the Dee in full spate took, and still takes, a short cut across the horseshoe-shaped field. The silt deposited by this river water acted like modern fertilisers and ensured a good crop of grass the following year. The hay on this low-lying land was harvested rather later than on the higher ground, which made it more convenient to borrow horses and mowing machines from those who had already brought their hay in. Late June meant early rising for these tough, hard-working men. Having to keep up their normal employment entailed mowing the hay before going to work, and it was not at all unusual to hear the machines going long before day-break. The hay, when harvested properly, was some of the best around, and any surplus was sold to owners of hunting horses, being ideal for this purpose.

Several families would work together as a team to load and cart the hay. One of the vanished sights of the countryside was men, women and children working in the hayfield to gather the crop by the sweat of their brow, yet a joyful atmosphere would prevail. Some of the crop would be stored in small buildings close to the house called hay bays, one of which is still in existence, some in lofts over the buildings which housed the cattle. There were no bales or balers, so all the hay was carried from the field loose, after being worked by hand with rakes and "pikels" (pitchforks) until in the right condition to carry.

As the years passed the small-scale operations of the estate workers became no longer viable and farm produce was purchased from the small farms, many of them only too willing to sell milk, eggs and butter. This meant that the town fields and Radley Meadow were less in demand and gradually the smaller farms took over an acre here and an acre there in these communal fields. Several of the older employees were reluctant to give up their holding and for a number of years carried on growing crops for sale, having given up keeping a milking cow or bacon pig. Potatoes were the main crop grown then; they needed less labour than the other root crops and were fairly easy to sell. One old lad grew half an acre of vegetable marrows – goodness knows

7

what for, but what a crop! As the story has it, you needed a cross-cut saw before you could load them on a cart. Being a wily old lad, he no doubt had a market for such tremendous specimens; probably they went to a nearby factory for processing.

Several of these acres were still occupied by the cottagers at the end of the second world war, and a number still held a patch on Radley Meadow, but the milking cows had gone and only "dry" stock was kept. Yearling heifer calves were bought in and reared until it was time for them to go to the bull, or occasionally they would be taken to a local farmer's bull and then sold on the point of calving, just coming into profit as they said. There was not much interest about pedigrees among the small farms in those days. The reputation of the farmer was good enough to sell in-calf beasts, and a heifer in calf to "Farmer George's bull" would ensure a good price. By the early nineteen-fifties all the small-time operations had ceased, and the town fields, Radley Meadow and the ley field had been absorbed into the smaller farms, most of which were glad of a few extra acres in the changing economic climate. Even with the extra land, the six small farms in the village of Aldford still averaged only around seventy acres, barely large enough to justify the employment of one hired hand. These farm labourers had to be able to turn their hand to many jobs and were in fact highly skilled: good horsemen, good ploughmen, good cowmen, good at hedge-cutting, hedge-laying and fencing, draining and in fact any job that cropped up on a small farm, even to plucking and dressing turkeys and geese for the Christmas market. To a large extent these are a lost race of men, since modern farming needs specialists and few are good at all the skills required.

There were also many larger farms on Eaton Estate, mostly around the two-hundred-acre mark. These farms employed several men each, the number depending on the type of husbandry. Cheshire being largely a dairy county, milk production was the main activity. Some corn was grown where the land was lighter, but most farmers relied on a good crop of hay for the winter feed. The actual farming practices were much different in those days. For example, all

8

the milking was done by hand and most farm labourers' wives had to assist in this task morning and night. Usually this entailed working from six to eight in the morning and four to six in the afternoon – not much time left for gallivanting! The pay for this seven-days-a-week task was only a pittance, and the men's wages were always low: about thirty-six shillings a week in the nineteen-thirties, with no overtime pay and no holidays. If a man did take a week off there was usually no pay, unless the boss was a particularly generous man. Harvesting was all part of the year's work, but if the harvest was good the farmer was often more generous with his "harvest money". This was the only cash the labourer received above his weekly wage, and even then seldom exceeded two pounds.

Many children from country villages rarely visited a town. Maybe the choir outing, an annual event, was the only time they went out of their village, so they had to make their own amusement and seek their own pleasures. This lack of real mobility ensured that in many cases, son followed in father's footsteps and worked at one job or another on the Eaton Estate or on the tenanted farms. Sometimes as many as three generations of the same family would be employed on farm or estate. In those days, retirement didn't happen at sixty-five; many an old "lad" was still working into his seventies, and doing a good day's work too. Today there appear to be only two father and son combinations working in the area: George Cotton and his son Alan, both working in the forestry department, and Jim Fairbanks and his son Clifford on the home farm. There is no doubt that continuity of service is a good thing for most occupations on both estate and farm, since it helps to keep that bond between employer and employee which really does mean so much. The worker often knows what the boss wants before the boss himself!

Of course, if the employer is never satisfied but always complaining and picking on the workers, it is inevitable that there will be a pretty frequent change-over of the labour force. Personal contact is very important where there are only small staffs employed, and years ago, when a farmer advertised at frequent intervals for, maybe, a cowman, ploughman or shepherd, it became well known that he was

9

not a good employer. Thus he only got workers who weren't really skilled or who maybe knew little about farm work but were really desperate for a house to live in. Some of these farmers were often excellent in other ways but somehow had the knack of upsetting the workers, some were hard task-masters and some even insulting. The story goes that one farmer had just taken on a new hand, round about hay-making time, and first thing in the morning came out onto the yard to give orders for the day. The weather was hardly fit for haymaking, being a bit on the damp side, so he told the man that after he had milked the cows, fifty of them, and fed the pigs and hens, he must go to a field a mile away and look at the heifers to see that they were all right, then when he got back he must go and hoe an acre of turnips and then he could get about ten hundredweight of "tatties" up, ready for market the next day. "It should have cleared up by then," said the farmer, "so you'll be able to go and row in that ten acres of hay in the Glebe field."

The farmhand looked at him dumbstruck, and as the farmer turned away said, "Where's the pan shovel, boss?"

"What do you want the shovel for?" asks the farmer.

"Well, by the time I've done all those jobs, there'll be some snow to shift!"

This is probably only a good story, but it is true to the way things could be in those days. Yet despite all these hardships the men of the land were always a cheerful band and enjoyed their work. There were obviously a few perks: a free cottage, free milk, often a dozen eggs at the week-end, sometimes a pat of butter or a piece of cheese.

A number of the larger farms made cheese in those days, the famous farmhouse Cheshire cheese, a rare commodity now and much more appetising than the modern factory-made "Cheshire". Each farm had its own cheesemaker, whose responsibility was solely to produce good cheese, and who rarely had any other tasks to perform but lived on the farm as part of the farmer's household.

Today cheese is made in a cheese factory from the milk collected from a large number of farms, whereas in earlier days each farm produced its own individual type of cheese. The type of herbage on the particular farm made all the difference to the end product, as did the time of year the cheese was made. Different parts of Cheshire had different flavours to their cheeses, as in fact did different fields on each farm. As the cheese was made every day, one farm could produce several quite different-flavoured cheeses. Because the land had been grassland for several generations, there were varied types of herbage in each field. Some were with and some without the wild white clover, and others had different types of what today are called weeds, but all contributed to the production of milk and to the subtle flavours in the cheese produced from that milk. September was reckoned on most farms to produce the best cheese, which would be in prime condition for the Christmas market, although the cheese-making season on most farms in those days ran from April, when the cows were turned out to grass, until early October, when they were brought into the shippons for the winter. Thousands of tons of cheese must have been produced on the farms in the days before the war, but now the number of farmers making cheese in Cheshire has been reduced to a mere handful. There was a great demand for the farmhouse cheese and on one occasion, when a local farmer was asked if he had any cheese for sale, he replied, "No, master, I h'aint. The Duke's eaten all", a pun on the Duke of Westminster owning Eaton Hall!

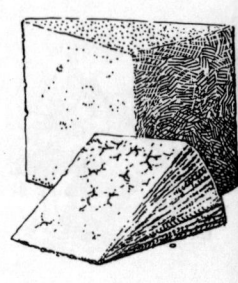

Today the cheese seems too fresh, and even the so-called mature cheese is a poor shadow of those pre-war products. It was the custom to keep the cheeses, which were quite large, about fifty-six pounds each, in the "cheese room", a large airy room often up a flight of stairs. The cheeses were turned every day to ensure an even distribution of moisture, and it was rare for a cheese to be sold to the cheese factory before it was two or even three months old. Most farmers had the cheesemakers make several small cheeses, around seven pounds in weight, at certain times of the year. These were kept for their own use, and one or two were stored for a long period until the cheese had streaks of blue and became the oh! so tasty and appetising "Cheshire blue".

Milk production dropped during the winter months and, with the cattle being housebound, was not quite as suitable for making cheese. It was sold as liquid milk, being collected

11

daily or even taken to the nearest railway station in "tankards". Things were so timed that the bulk of the cattle calved in the spring, thus ensuring a good flush of milk when the grass was growing and, as the farmers said, "keep was cheap".

There was a saying that it was a poor farm that wouldn't keep one idle man, but that was usually the excuse a farmer gave when he was having a day away from the farming chores. Those chores were always many and varied. For example, after the cattle had been taken into the buildings for the winter, it was the time to manure the land. There were no man-made fertilisers in the nineteen-thirties and this task was all done by hand. Horses and carts were mobilised and sometimes several farmers would help one another with men and tackle. With men loading the carts at the midden, men leading the carts and unloading them on the fields, it was a time of great activity in the countryside.

The midden was the storage place for the previous winter's manure from the shippons and on large farms would hold several hundred tons of manure, all of it to be moved by hand three times. After nine months in the midden the manure was well rotted and gave off an aroma all of its own, and by the time it had been loaded and unloaded into "cobs" on the field, a large area was filled with this healthy smell! The cobs were heaps of manure pulled off the cart with a special tool, a muck hook, and were spaced over the field at given intervals and to a certain size. This controlled the amount of manure on any one field, which varied according to the type of land and what was required from it. A field that was going to be mown for hay usually got a larger dressing than one to be used for grazing only, to ensure a good crop of hay followed by a good "head-ish" (young grass) for turning the cattle on in the autumn.

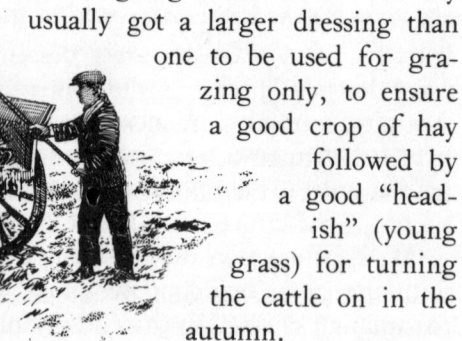

Once the midden was empty came the task of muckspreading. Frequently Irishmen who had been on the farms helping with the harvest would do this on a piece-work basis, getting maybe a farthing a cob. This meant hard work to get a good week's wages! The spreading of the manure meant plenty of easy feed for the small birds and these would follow the men at a safe distance as the cobs were spread. With plenty of insects available. flocks of birds could be seen on each field. Admittedly the majority were starlings, but on closer observation many other species were to be seen: several varieties of the wagtail family, the great tits, the blue tits, even members of the seed-eating tribes, chaffinches, the odd bullfinch and, when the field was near to habitation, the common house sparrow. The seagulls rarely descended on a field that had been mucked, preferring to follow the plough as they do to this day, but alas, modern spreading of manure does not attract the quantity of small birds it did in the past. In fact, are there the same number of small birds about? Not as far as I can see.

The autumn and winter were the seasons to see to the hedges and ditches and to attend to any area that needed draining. The larger farms usually had a man well-skilled in one or more of these essential tasks. Many fields had a pit or pond, the well-known Cheshire marl pits. These pits served a most useful purpose. They had been made by the soil (marl) being taken out and spread on the land as fertiliser; this must have involved many hours of toil, all by hand, since some of the pits covered almost half an acre and were six to eight feet in depth. When completed, the pit was allowed to fill with water and became the watering-place for livestock grazing that particular field. The subsoil in most parts of the Cheshire Plain is very heavy, frequently clay, so once the pit was full, a water supply was available at all times, even in a very hot, dry summer. The sides of the pits were gently sloped so that there was no danger to watering cattle, and eventually rushes, rough grass and other water-loving plants grew in the shallow surrounds. This made an ideal habitat for many species of water-loving insects and birds, from the mosquito and dragonfly to the moorhen and sedge warbler (pit sparrow) and, on the large pits, even the little grebe, called in Cheshire "tommy pudden" – goodness knows why! Over the years many of the pits had fish introduced into them, probably by the farmers' children, and even today give a lot of sport for the country children. The pits are way out in the fields so provide a relatively safe pastime for the younger generation and a good introduction into the sport of angling.

These pits were also used in many cases as a drainage sump for the field, and the drains needed regular attention in order to function satisfactorily. The old hands were very skilled at this task, being able almost by instinct to tell where a drain was blocked and, by digging down to the drain at that spot, to release the held-up water. Every pit still has an overflow drain on the appropriate side which lets the surplus water off during a wet spell. These outlets needed attention every winter after being trampled over by the cattle during the summer. The old hands knew exactly where to look and, by taking up a couple of pipes or so and re-laying them, made sure that the pit was kept at a more or less constant level.

Re-draining a field was a really skilled job, but the old-timers could do it without the modern instruments to take levels, and many drains laid by these men even a hundred years ago are still working as well as when they were laid. All the work was done by hand. After it had been decided where the drain should run, a few sticks were stuck up to mark the line and then a trench one "spit" (spade-depth) deep was taken out and put carefully on one side with the grass uppermost. The rest of the soil taken out was put on the other side, and after the drain had been laid and the soil replaced with the grass "sod" on top, it wasn't long before it had settled and merged into the surroundings.

Several different types of spade were used in this process: a grafting spade for the first trench, a narrower spade called a draining tool to get down to the required depth, and then at pipe level a swan-neck, which describes it exactly. These swan-necks came in various sizes, depending on the size of drain, but were usually three or four inches in diameter. Used correctly, this tool made a curved bed for the tile pipe to rest in. Even today some of the yet older drains are come across – these are "horseshoe" drains, very often set on a slate base to prevent them sinking and to facilitate the flow of water. A far cry from the modern plastic machine-laid pipes! Will they be working in a hundred years?

At one time the ditches which are around most fields on the Cheshire dairy-farm belt were cleaned out every winter, since they were the course which the water from many field drains had to take, including the pit overflows. This was not such a skilled job as laying drains, but still required a good eye to make sure that not too much was taken out of the bottom of the ditch, causing the water to lie in one spot.

The hedges are always an important factor in dairy farming and in bygone days these hedges were trimmed by hand, using various types of brushing hook. These tools, some long-bladed, some short and some curved, were always kept very sharp and, used by an expert, could trim a hedge as well as the modern machinery. Different workers used different hooks but the real experts had a tool for each type of hedge, according to the formation, height, width and growth. "Watty" Huxley was the real expert at hedge-cutting. There were many miles of hedges to be trimmed on Eaton Estate each autumn and Watty was usually in charge of the gang to do this job. The younger lads had the task of "copping", that is cleaning the base of the hedge with either a copping hook or a scythe, while other woodmen brushed the sides of the hedge. But it was usually Watty who cut the top. He had a special style of his own, swinging the razor-sharp hook over his head in a circle. The top had to be absolutely level, not like a switchback, and there was no doubt about it being level when Watty had cut it. Pride in the job was what counted. Those old lads certainly had that, and instilled it in the younger members of the gang.

A certain number of hedges were left to grow up each year. These were due to be "laid". This was done when a hedge was getting thin in the bottom and there were gaps appearing so that it was no longer good enough to keep cattle in. The hedges were left to grow for several years until they had reached a height of eight or nine feet, which was an ideal height for laying. The operation of laying consisted of cleaning out the dead and weak growth in the hedge and then half-cutting through the tall, sturdy growth and laying it at an angle to the ground, forming a solid fence. Each layer was interwoven round stakes driven into the ground, and then trimmed to present a neat and tidy appearance.

There are several methods of hedge-laying, usually connected with the type of farm – cattle, sheep or arable. There can even be various methods used on a single farm. Where cattle will be using the fields it is normal to lay "on the layers", that is each piece on top of the other, forming a sturdy hedge. In sheep country more brush than growth is left on, making it a thicker barrier, but in arable areas the hedge is laid "off the layers". These arable-country hedges are seldom trimmed, but a new hedge is allowed to grow from the basic cuts of the layers. Then, after eight or ten years according to the growth made, the old layers are cut out and the process starts again.

Watty Huxley spent most winters hedge-laying, sometimes on the woodland hedges and sometimes on loan to a tenant farmer. Not all farmworkers would take on the task of laying a hedge, so Watty was fully employed most winters at the task he probably liked the best. Many miles of hedges on Eaton Estate, even today after forty or more years, are proof of his exceptional skill. Fortunately, Watty trained one or two younger men and even today, odd short lengths of hedge are laid.

The art of hedge-laying has always been a rather competitive business and each year, usually in November, most counties held ploughing and hedging matches. These matches were purely and simply competitions for men who worked on the land, giving them an opportunity to show off their skills; as the prizes were small, it was really a matter of pride in the work. Today the hedge-laying competitions are much the same, starting at novices through to the open class, open to all-comers.

Watty Huxley started in the novice class, soon becoming first-prize winner, then winning the County class and shortly after, winning the open class against all-comers. Watty eventually won all prizes available to him, and in his latter years became a judge at the hedge-laying competitions, travelling to various venues. His cottage was bursting at the seams with all the awards he had received, from salvers to rosettes.

Modern ploughing and hedging matches, like so many other things, seem to have become commercialised, with trade stands extolling the benefits of this or that machine. As one horse-loving farmer said at one of these events recently, "They come round and persuade you to buy a tractor that will plough an acre in less time than the one you've got, at a cost of £20,000-plus. Then the next year they try to get you to buy a machine to break up the soil which the heavy and expensive tractor has compacted so hard that the land is waterlogged!"

He was obviously not too impressed with modern machinery, and Watty Huxley would not have been impressed with the modern hedge-cutting implements either. Nothing can stand still for too long, and the modern hedge-cutting machinery can cut a lot of hedge in a day, chewing the cuttings into small pieces which do not need cleaning up, except from the roads. But the various types of tractor-driven hedge-cutter are all noisy and the operator has to be in a cab, protected from flying pieces of hedge. Although a degree of skill is needed to use a machine of this type, it cannot be compared with the flashing blade of the old-timer. The

economics of modern farming no doubt make it essential to
use such mechanical devices, but the old skill and closeness to
nature have gone.

2

By the outbreak of the second world war in 1939, most of the cottagers' land had gone to the smaller farms, increasing their acreage slightly, but this redistribution did not always improve these farms of seventy or eighty acres. The cottagers' land was spread over quite a large area, and despite all attempts at re-organisation, it meant that some farmers had land at a distance from their main holding. This did not lead to efficient farming and gradually, as the older tenant farmers died, their holdings were absorbed either by Eaton home farm or by larger farms with adjacent land.

Eventually, in the village of Aldford, which before 1939 had six farms of seventy or so acres, none remained. With this change, the town fields, Radley Meadow and the ley field were taken over by the home farm. This altered the character of the village and, with the same changes taking place on other villages on the estate, the character of the estate itself. Gone were characters like Horace Lewis of Oak Tree Farm, Albert Thomas of Green Lake Farm and "Pop" Clarke of Ford Lane. All these hard-working men had little to show for a lifetime's work in the end, and even their sons were

19

unable to carry on the family farming interests. Such small farms were simply no longer viable propositions under the conditions of that time in Cheshire. Even some of the larger farms were merged, making holdings of four to five hundred acres.

With these changes there were also changes in the number of men employed on the land. Fifty years ago, even the small farms usually had work for three men, often the farmer and his son with one hired hand. With modern machinery and implements, very few staff are needed to work vast tracts of land. Whereas about forty men worked on the farms in the vicinity of Aldford before the war, now seven or eight men work the same area! It must be viable, but what a change it has made to the countryside and to life in the villages. There have also been many changes in the crops grown; oats was the main pre-war corn crop, with a small amount of wheat, but in the nineteen-seventies a swing to barley became obvious. Some farms remain basically dairy farms but where the land is suitable grow some corn, which no doubt helps to offset the very high price of compounded feeds.

With the swing to larger farming units came the tendency for larger fields, which meant the removing of many hedgerows. This in itself has completely altered the character of the landscape around Aldford and in other parts of Cheshire. With the larger machines of all descriptions, larger fields must be a great attraction, but what effect will this wholesale removing of hedges have on the environment in general? True, the big tractors and machinery can work many acres of land in a day, be it ploughing, sowing or combine-harvesting the crops, but the long-term outcome remains to be seen. The very fact that all the implements used on the land are much heavier than they were, and in fact tend to get larger and more powerful, has an effect on the soil never known before. Although they work the surface quickly and efficiently, the subsoil appears to be compacted more and more and some land that has had good natural drainage, probably for centuries, now gets waterlogged after even a comparatively light rainfall. As that farmer said at the ploughing match, "More expensive machinery next year to put that right."

I have already described how well-rotted manure was spread on the land by hand before the war. Today it is rare, at least in Cheshire, to see matured manure. The modern methods of handling dairy stock mean that all the so-called manure is pushed mechanically into a "lagoon" (a large hole excavated for the purpose) and then eventually spread on the land in more or less liquid form. This so-called manure appears to be another agent in compacting what was quite light soil.

In addition to these methods, artificial fertilisers of endless variety are used to improve productivity and, as far as it is possible to judge, in ever-increasing quantities. This use of fertilisers is demanded by what is now a universal method of providing winter cattle-feed, silage-making. To ensure a good crop of grass early, some form of nitrogen is essential and that is where the fertiliser comes in. Often two cuts of grass are taken off each field being used for silage-making, which entails further dressings of chemicals.

What effect have all these changes, although comparatively gradual, had on the environment and on wildlife in particular? Many small birds which in the nineteen-thirties were plentiful do not seem to be about in the same numbers, and even some of the larger ones, for instance the corncrake.  Fifty years ago this bird was quite common in Cheshire and bred freely in many parts, but not for some time. A pair did appear in 1977 on the outskirts of Aldford but there is some doubt whether they bred or not, owing to silage-making on the field they occupied.

The grasshopper warbler is another summer visitor seldom heard these days, whereas at one time it was not at all unusual to hear several birds with that distinctive call in a comparatively small area. Plovers abounded, and nested not only on the water meadows but on the cornfields of the higher land; it was a sure sign that spring was not far off when the peewit started its nuptial display. Today in the early spring just a few pairs are wheeling and diving over the meadows with that rather plaintive call they have.

Many of these less numerous birds are insect-eaters, and there must be a link with the destruction of hedges: apart from the fact that there are less nesting sites, insects must

21

have been reduced drastically. That's the effect on the insect-eating birds, but one would think that with much more grain being grown, the seed-eating birds would be on the increase. Of course, many seed-eaters do not take feed the size of wheat or barley, but even the large birds that do have diminished in numbers. The rook in particular is not as common as in the past, although it is a bird that can eat many things. Many sites of long-established rookeries have been lost to Dutch elm disease, but rooks will nest in almost any tall group of trees, so that factor is most unlikely to affect numbers. Fertilisers and sprays have taken their toll.

Pigeons, although still around in fairly large numbers, are nowhere near as numerous as in the past. Before the war, when shoots were organised to reduce the huge flocks, it was not uncommon for one man to get fifty or sixty birds, and with maybe forty guns out on an estate the size of Eaton (twelve thousand acres), vast numbers of birds were killed in the four nights usually allotted. Yet there were as many as ever around the next year. Today, it is very doubtful if forty guns would kill more than two hundred pigeons. A couple of miles south of Aldford is the well-known Dee valley market garden area, and if there are many pigeons about, steps have to be taken to protect the valuable crops, either by shooting or by the use of automatic bird-scarers. For quite a few years now, no such activity has been heard in that area, a sure sign that pigeons are not so numerous. The severe winter of 1963 decimated the pigeon flocks as it did many other species, but although the pigeon stock increased rapidly in the ensuing years, it now seems to be on the wane again in this south-west corner of Cheshire.

A comparative newcomer belonging to the same family as the pigeon (ring dove), the collared dove, is on the increase, however. Having come over, or been brought over, from the Continent, it has spread north and is very common indeed at Eaton. Unlike its cousin, the collared dove prefers to spend its time close to habitation, and for a large part of the year its rather monotonous call has become very familiar and even boring.

A lot of the birds of prey have also suffered badly from various forms of pollution. Sparrow hawks were very scarce at one time but now seem to have recovered; maybe the increase in collared doves has been a factor, since they make easy prey for the darting, swooping hawk. A few years ago,  some of the sprays used on agricultural land were blamed for the decline of the sparrow hawk and the kestrel population, and it is certain that at that time it was not uncommon for breeding birds of those species to rear only one or two chicks instead of the usual four or more; some pairs did not even rear any. Fortunately, with a change in the type of sprays used, these magnificent birds of the countryside are once again at least holding their own.

Somehow, when other wildlife suffers from man's inter-ference with the environment, there is one bird that seems to prosper and increase in numbers, namely that villain of the feathered world, the carrion crow. There appear to be more in the countryside than ever, and some have even taken to frequenting more urban areas — quite recently a pair were observed close to the County Police Headquarters in Chester, where an old nest could be seen in the fork of a tree, right amongst the noise and fumes of an ever-increasing flow of traffic. Maybe this bird, being adapted to feeding on carrion as its name implies, is more able to deal with modern pollution.

Not only has the feathered population of the countryside suffered and changed. Fifty years ago, grasshoppers abounded and made a now almost unknown chorus in the long grass at certain times of the year. Some old characters maintained they could forecast the weather by the way these insects acted, and by gum they were very often spot on! Butterflies were abundant, attracted by the variety of plants in the fields and hedges. Many varieties no longer seen made a splash of colour fluttering back and to across the swaying grass and hedges. The common cabbage white butterfly seems to be about the only one to be seen in any numbers these days, but a few places, mostly the undisturbed patches, still have small numbers of the meadow brown and common blue. Even the various types of dragonflies seem less numerous, but somehow the mosquito and midge have survived, to torment man on a humid summer evening.

There have been a lot of changes in the wild mammal life as well. It is well known that myxomatosis decimated the rabbits in almost all parts of the United Kingdom, but how many other inhabitants of the field and woods were affected by the widespread plague? It doesn't appear as if foxes were greatly diminished by this loss of apparently abundant food. It is doubtful if they ever killed as many rabbits for food as was imagined, although many young rabbits were certainly dug out of "stops" away from burrows, and probably the doe often taken as well. This happened only over a short period each year, when both rabbits and foxes were breeding, and in any case a vixen with hungry cubs to feed is not particular what the food is. Often the remains of many things can be seen in an earth with cubs in residence – domestic hens, rabbits, hares, pheasant, partridge, water-hens and even young rooks (the rooks after falling from their nests). With such a varied diet, Reynard did not miss the rabbit too much and soon adapted his taste in the way of food.

The badger will take a few young rabbits but really is much more inclined to exist on a different type of diet, being very fond of digging wasps' nests out of the ground for the pupae and not averse to a few eggs taken from ground-

nesting birds. Beetles are a great favourite of Brock and it is not at all unusual to see where he has been turning cow-pats over to get at the beetles beneath. The loss of the rabbit affected the badger but little, and probably the modern means of transport have done more damage than anything to this very interesting denizen of the English countryside. Fifty years ago, with motor cars in rural areas practically non-existent, it was unknown to find a dead badger by the roadside. Having a network of runs throughout the country, badgers cross roads and lanes in more or less well-defined spots, and it is at these places that so many of them now come to an untimely end. In Aldford and its surrounding villages, several badgers each year, sometimes as many as six, are known to meet their deaths by fast-moving traffic. Fortunately badgers are still fairly plentiful in this area, but if five or six a year are killed on about ten miles of roads, what must the grand total throughout the country be?

The disappearance, more or less, of the rabbits certainly made a difference to the people living in the country. The farmers were obviously pleased to see the coney drastically reduced in numbers, for without doubt much grass and corn was eaten by the pre-war hordes of them. Still, some farmers probably had rather mixed feelings because the humble rabbit provided many a good feed for country people and the farmers, most of whom liked a bit of rural sport, looked forward to a day's ferreting. Eaton being a sporting estate, these ferreting days were properly organised, particularly if the rabbits were to be shot, and as a rule one or two of the estate keepers were present, providing the ferrets and working them. No shooting was allowed close to the coverts, which in those days held a huge stock of pheasants, so farmers having land next to these woods had to wait until the end of the shooting season before they could shoot rabbits – or anything else for that matter – on their land. They still got their day's sport, for it was the custom to have at least four shooting in a ferreting party. On the larger farms, two parties would often be out, so those with farms where shooting was not allowed until February were guests on the farms on the outskirts of the estate. When February came the roles were reversed. It was not unusual for some of the farmers keen on shooting to have a day's ferreting almost every week from October to March, and this activity played a great part in controlling the rabbit population.

A lot of leg-pulling went on in those days, for some of the farmers were good shots while others couldn't hit a haystack, but the day's sport was the main thing. It was designed to be a day out with a purpose, and it was rare that the cash obtained from the sale of the rabbits didn't cover the outlay by the farmer for entertaining his guests. Large numbers were often killed in one day, depending on the size of the farm and the type of land, but on one farm it was not at all unusual to take more than two hundred coney. At tenpence to a shilling each, the income adequately covered what, even in those days, was lavish entertaining.

It was usual for the party to meet at the farm for breakfast, which by any standards was adequate. Having started ferreting at about ten, coffee or tea, laced with something a bit stronger, would be brought out soon after eleven by the maids (most farms employed a maid in those days). About twelve-thirty lunch would arrive, and this tended to vary according to the time of year. It could be soup, pies or sandwiches followed by fruit tart and cream or maybe hotpot, with real Cheshire cheese and more than likely home-baked bread. This meal was eaten wherever the ferreting party happened to be, sitting on the ferret boxes or nearby railings. When the day came to an end the party adjourned to the farmhouse, where another meal was laid on! It was all in a day's sport.

Certainly in Cheshire, days like that no longer take place, and even if the rabbit population should ever increase to the density of the nineteen-thirties, it is much more likely that they would be gassed than shot bolting from ferrets.

Not only the farmers had sport with rabbits, but the farm labourers also. Where corn was grown, great fun was had as the last few swaths were cut. Rabbits would start to leave their rapidly diminishing habitat, only to be chased by farm-workers armed with sticks, and many a chap has received a blow from a stick wielded by a zealous youth! Where large numbers were known to be in a field of corn, the keepers were often called in to set long nets round the perimeter to catch the rabbits as they attempted to escape, and with the farm men chasing them, very few coneys got away. It was rather warm work on a blazing August day, but all part of the lost rural scene.

As a gamekeeper had to be present when all these activities took place, we saw many amusing incidents. On one occasion a small farm was having its usual day after rabbits, and as it was a farm with a comparatively small number of coneys, only the farmer and his neighbour were shooting. It was a very pleasant day in early spring, and towards midday an elderly figure appeared, the father of the tenant farmer, known to one and all as "Grandad". It was most unusual to see him out in the fields at his ripe old age, but this time the weather had enticed him and what was more, he was carrying a gun. He said, "I've come to show you young 'uns how to shoot. You've been having two or three shots at every rabbit that's shown its face." Fair enough, because these small-time farmers rarely used a gun and were not very adept at shoot-

ing a fast-moving, dodging rabbit. Grandad took up a suitable position, and it wasn't long before a target presented itself. Raising his single-barrelled gun to his shoulder, he pulled the trigger and bunny rolled over, clean killed, much to the surprise of those present! Grandad was then observed to be rubbing his eyes and, on being asked what was the matter, replied, "It's the danged woodworm in the stock. Filled my eyes with dust." On inspecting the gun, the keeper bluntly refused to carry on if another shot was fired from the ancient gun – it was undoubtedly in an unfit condition and a danger not only to the user but to others present as well. Grandad wasn't a bit amused, saying, "I've had that 'bund hook' [gun] for sixty years. Why ain't it safe now?" However, his son prevailed and the poor old chap made his way back to the farmhouse in a huff.

A lot of people in the country were fond of a day after rabbits, and not least the local police officers. In those days most villages or groups of villages had their local resident "bobby", who patrolled his beat on a cycle. One day the gamekeepers were busy rabbiting along a roadside hedge when the local bobby appeared, no doubt having heard the shooting. Soon the rabbits ceased to bolt and it was decided to use a line ferret and dig as many as possible out. The bobby leant on his bike watching, but after a while he could stand it no longer and, throwing off his cape, grabbed a spade and helped in the digging. It wasn't long before his uniform was plastered with mud, but this did not deter him at all – he was enjoying himself! Eventually the keepers decided to move to another burrow, leaving the policeman to carry on with his self-imposed task, and shortly another portly figure in blue appeared on a cycle. It was the section sergeant. A whistle warned the mud-covered bobby of his approaching superior, but no matter, he kept on digging. The sergeant duly arrived and after a few words with the labouring officer, he too joined in the digging after rabbits! Soon the sergeant was on his knees, pulling the rabbits from the burrow, and also caked in mud. Lunchtime arrived and the whole party adjourned to a nearby pub where the landlord supplied a ploughman's lunch and the policemen made themselves more presentable before resuming duty. They did not leave empty-handed, but took a couple of rabbits apiece for a future meal! This couldn't happen today, but was typical of the easy-going way of life in the countryside that has vanished.

The gamekeepers had the responsibility of keeping the rabbits within reasonable numbers all over a large estate and, when a large number of rabbits were left despite the winter ferreting activities, resorted to trapping them. By the use of traps that have been illegal since the mid-nineteen-fifties, hundreds of rabbits were prevented from doing damage to the spring corn. In a way it was a rather cruel method of dealing with the so-called pest. A number of traps were set in each burrow or warren and all other exits securely stopped to prevent the occupants escaping. Pushing old newspaper down the hole before filling it with soil made it more difficult for the occupants to escape; as one old keeper said, "Give 'em something to read." It certainly prevented bunny from escaping, but when one decided to leave through the hole in which the trap was set, that was the cruel part of

the operation. Although the gamekeepers did their best to prevent suffering by visiting the traps at least twice a day, it was inevitable that some rabbits, often trapped by only one leg, suffered to a considerable degree.

The traps were left in the burrow for five or six days, and even then some coneys would not face the traps. Towards the end of this period any rabbits trapped had lost all their fat and a considerable weight as well. Often the flesh would have a purple tinge, useless for sale and fit only to be fed to the ferrets or dogs. It is not illegal to trap rabbits today, so long as a so-called "humane" trap is used. The "juby" trap is not as efficient at catching coneys as the old gin-trap and, being less easy to handle, is seldom used, at least in Cheshire. Despite the quite high prices paid for wild rabbits, Cymag is nearly always used should rabbits build up to an unacceptable number, and doubtless this gassing is a viable way of control.

In the early nineteen-thirties, Eaton Estate like many others abounded with hares, although it is said that it is rare to find large numbers of hares where there are also large numbers of rabbits. This was not true of Eaton, where both flourished, and their abundance was taken advantage of by several trainers of greyhounds whose establishments were within a reasonable distance. Major Basil Kerr, the agent for the estate at that time, was very interested in coursing and had connections with the blue riband of coursing, the Waterloo Cup, which was held annually at Altcar, near Liverpool. So the greyhound trainers had permission to hold trials of their charges on certain parts of the estate, provided as always that gamekeepers were present. Harold Wright was probably the best-known trainer of those days, having trained several winners of the coveted highest accolade of coursing, and many of those greyhounds were trained on Eaton hares. Many of these trials had to take place in great secrecy, as it was most important that other interested parties were not aware of the abilities of a particular greyhound. Betting being an important part, particularly of the coursing meetings held on Lord Sefton's estate at Altcar, the less people knew of a dog's skill, as with horse-racing, the better for the informed punters. Usually the training trials were held in

places where it was most difficult to see what was going on

from a public highway, and frequently at pretty short notice, thus maintaining at least a fair degree of secrecy.

Shortly after the second world war, a coursing club was formed, the Eaton Coursing Club, and for a number of years meetings were held annually on the Eaton Estate. On the death of Major Basil Kerr, the estate agent and leading light in the club, interest started to wane to a certain degree. Mrs Basil Kerr was also very interested in coursing and owned a greyhound, Jonquil, which won the Waterloo Cup, but despite the efforts of a number of interested local farmers, and mainly due to the change in farming operations, the club eventually folded.

Hares today are no longer plentiful, in fact in places quite scarce, but in the nineteen-thirties there had to be some control of such a large number of hares, and this took basic-ally two forms. Immediately after the Waterloo Cup meeting in February, it was usual for the gamekeepers from Lord Sefton's estate at Altcar to come over to Eaton and assist the Eaton keepers in the netting of hares. When caught, those  hares were transported to Altcar in specially made boxes and released on the coursing grounds there. The object was two-fold: to "change the blood" of the resident Altcar hares, and of course to increase the numbers there. It was not at all unusual to net up to a hundred and fifty hares on one of those days, but even that did not make much impression on the number of hares on the ground. To reduce the numbers further, several days of hare driving and shooting were organised over various parts of the estate, which did a lot to keep the hare population under control. Sometimes more than two hundred hares would be killed in a day which, with the netting of live hares for Altcar, gives some indication of the number on the ground in those days.

Once again, modern farming methods are probably the cause of the decline in the hare population in this part of Cheshire. So much silage is made during early summer, when many leverets are born, that there is little chance for them to survive the fast-moving, whirring machines. This means that no special effort has to be made to control the hare these days, although some areas get the attention of poachers from the towns, who come onto the land with whippets, lurchers and greyhounds to course what hares they can find. These visitors are not at all popular with the farmers, disturbing cattle and sheep as they do, and not infrequently leaving gates open and breaking down fences. These visitors were practically unheard of during the 'thirties, apart from the occasional hare taken by any gipsies that may have been in the vicinity.

Gipsies are seldom seen in this area today, seeming to gather on allotted sites, and with their caravans motorised now, it is as if part of the old rural scene has vanished, no doubt forever. Gipsies usually had a bad name, but it is doubtful if they did half of what they were blamed for. Yes, they would take the odd hare or rabbit, a few potatoes and turnips, but probably no more than many a farm labourer did without giving it a thought. The Romanies would often call at suitable withen beds and cut a supply of wands for their traditional peg-making activities, but it took an expert and keen eye to see where they had been at work and the withens had been cut.

Maybe they still do these things today, but somehow the mystery and intrigue seem to have gone. Travelling the country in a motor car or van must make a difference to these

people. The horse-drawn caravan gave them much more opportunity to view the surrounding countryside and to observe the presence of game or other things that might interest them.

Usually these Romanies were moved on after twenty-four hours by the local policeman, and they knew there were few places where they could stay much longer. Travelling from one end of the country to the other meant a constant flow of the traditional ornamental caravans through the by-ways, and what a colourful sight that was on a bright spring morning. During the early summer, when the strawberries were ripe, a number of gipsies would congregate in the Farndon and Holt area of the Dee valley to be employed by the strawberry growers. It was only a short season, but no doubt well worth it to the travelling folk.

There used to be an influx of all sorts of unemployed people for this seasonal work. Some of the larger growers even had first world war army huts on their land to accommodate the casual workers. This temporary increase in the local population was a godsend to the tradesmen, and particularly the publicans! Even today there are still seven public houses to meet the needs of the two smallish villages. This seasonal crop attracted many visitors to the area, particularly at week-ends. Some would come by horse and trap, some by cycle, a few by motor car and more by bus. One character, who lived on the outskirts of Chester, had been fortunate and won thirty thousand pounds from the Irish Hospitals Sweep on the Grand National. He visited Farndon and Holt every day during the strawberry season. Hiring a taxi in Chester, he would proceed to Farndon, where he had friends – no doubt even more after winning that amount of money! There he would purchase as many two-pound baskets of strawberries as could be piled in the taxi. Making his way back to town and varying the route each day, he would give a basket of the luscious berries to anyone he saw. Visiting every pub on his route was normal, and the landlord and customers in the hostelry all received a basket of fruit. Any left on arrival in Chester he would distribute in the poorer areas of the town. He was one of the characters of those days, who used his good fortune in the way he saw best and no doubt enjoyed

it. He was getting on in years when good fortune came to him and, after three seasons of distributing his largesse, he became ill and passed on.

Today, although there are still market gardens and strawberry growers in the area, the marketing methods have changed and there is no longer an influx of casual labour. Some produce is sold at the gate, some goes to local shops, but more than likely the bulk is sold on the "pick your own" system. This applies not only to strawberries but to all soft fruits and to apples as well. Such is the change over the years, but the crops have still to be gathered and the modern way, with people picking their own, at least means that all that is gathered is sold. At the same time, townspeople enjoy the outing to the country and the children can usually eat as much as they like whilst in the fields!

Before the war, though, several of the smaller farms on Eaton Estate had stalls in the markets. One such farmer, "Pop" Clarke, had a stall in Birkenhead market. Now Birkenhead must be at least twenty miles from the land Pop farmed at Aldford but without fail, every Saturday the journey was made to sell the produce of the farm. There were always eggs and poultry, and most weeks during the winter months a pig was killed, which produced joints of meat and sausages. Vegetables of one sort or another were usually available, but mainly the type produced in the fields – potatoes, particularly early ones, and turnips of course. Going back to the killing of a pig, this was only done in those days when there was an "R" in the month. It was rare to eat pork during May, June, July and August, presumably because the freezing of food was not general, and pork is rather tricky to handle during hot weather. Bacon and ham were available, cured on the farm, and without a doubt very much better than the product available today. Individual attention beats mass production for quality any day, at least as far as farm food is concerned.

All these goods were taken that twenty miles or so by horse and "shandry" (a light lorry). It meant an early start to be in Birkenhead when the market opened. The market closed at nine pm in those days, and it must have been a weary journey back home. It is doubtful if the stall would have been sold out much before closing time, for the public had got into the habit of leaving their shopping till late in the evening, when many a bargain could be picked up; the traders by then had reduced prices to enable them to dispose of their wares, many of which were perishable.

Many of the villagers fifty years ago would deal with the local farmers for various commodities. It was very convenient to get a pound or two of home-made sausages or a nice piece of pork without having to journey into town, and there is no doubt that home-killed pork and the sausages were very tasty indeed. Today, with modern feeds and the so-called high conversion rate, the meat from the butcher's shop lacks a lot of flavour, compared to that from animals fed on probably more natural feeds. "High conversion rate" means producing more meat or milk from a given amount of feed, thus supposedly making the produce cheaper. Unfortunately this only appears to be so in theory – maybe the production rate is higher, but these products aren't exactly cheap, and oh, what a loss in quality!

Many a housewife made a small amount of butter by collecting the cream off a day or two's milk and putting it through a small glass churn or even shaking it in a large glass jar. The milk was collected daily by villagers who did not work on the farms – woodmen, foresters and the like – and many a schoolkid made his pocket money by fetching milk each evening and enjoyed doing it. Sometimes the menfolk would have to go for it when they got home. On one occasion, Harry Morgan, who worked as the train driver on the estate, had had a rather rough passage getting home from work. He lived in a cottage at the end of a lane a mile long, in fact called the Straight Mile. It was blowing a gale, at least force eight, and the rain was coming down in torrents. Although he had his cycle, it was almost impossible to ride into the wind so he had walked all the way. Arriving home tired, wet and bedraggled, Harry was looking forward to a hot meal and a rest by a blazing fire. As he opened the back door, he greeted his wife by saying, "Rose, it's not fit for a dog to be out." Back came the reply: "I know, Harry. Go to the farm and get the milk!" Harry was not very amused, but much better to go while he was still "rugged up" than to have to

turn out later and get wet again. It appears the usual milk lad had not turned up, and who could blame him on a night like that.

Today it is no longer possible to buy milk straight off the farms. Various authorities have seen to that. First the cattle had to be T.T. (tuberculin tested), and it took a long time for some farms to eradicate tuberculosis in their stock. Then all the milk had to be sold in sealed bottles, which meant more capital outlay for bottles etc. Although one or two farmers in the Aldford area did carry on, it wasn't very long before they began to give it up; with sales of only a gallon or two a day they were not making a profit, so eventually the larger dairies moved in and delivered milk to the whole area, pushing out any small man who had wanted to continue. At the start it was a seven days a week delivery from these large concerns, but now it is three or four days a week at the most, and certainly not on Saturdays or Sundays. By all accounts, if the Common Market had its way, everyone would have to get their milk from a shop! It might be a good idea if some of those law-makers had to travel a couple of miles or more to get their supply, preferably on foot through eighteen inches of snow. At least the dairies don't let folk down even under those conditions – they may be running a bit late, but they usually get through. However, even that kind of service doesn't improve the quality of the milk. After it has been collected in bulk tankers, mixed with other farms' milk and then put through various processes to give it so called "long life", there is no chance at all of a housewife making a bit of butter from the cream at the top of the bottle. It is very difficult to see any cream, and compared with the old type of milk, the whole lot is pretty thin.

Eggs were another item often purchased from local farms; although many of the country dwellers kept a few backyard hens, there were always some that didn't. Very often the cottagers' poultry was fed on household scraps with the minimum of grain, which was economical but did not make the hens very prolific with the eggs. During the spring and summer they would lay fairly well, but come the colder weather, egg-laying would practically cease. Then recourse was made to the farms, where larger numbers of birds were

36

kept which, being much better fed, would at least lay a few eggs during the winter months.

All the poultry were "free-range" and had freedom to roam more or less at will, particularly round the farm stack-yard where there was always plenty of picking. Naturally, some of the hens took advantage of this freedom and laid away from home, home being the nesting-boxes always provided in the hen-houses. Collecting the eggs from these outside nests could be a time-consuming job, for after a nest had been found and the eggs taken, the hen would frequently seek a new site to lay again. The farmer's wife usually had the egg money, although the feed for the poultry was provided out of the farm supplies. The lady of the house was therefore naturally very keen to gather all the eggs laid, and would often get the children who came for the evening milk to search the stackyard and buildings to find where the hens were laying. The usual reward for this was a lovely new-laid egg for the child's tea, so there was always some competition amongst the kids for this profitable chore.

Today very few of the large farms keep any poultry, unless of course they specialise in that branch of husbandry, and it is quite rare to see any cottage with a hen-pen. Travelling in a country district, you do occasionally see a sign up saying "Free-range eggs for sale", but it is an even bet that half of the eggs sold have come from deep-litter houses or battery cages. Often there are a few hens running about the yard, but also large huts where hens can be heard cackling! It is much more productive when the poultry are confined, and more profitable, but there isn't really any comparison between eggs from confined poultry and from free-range birds. They tell us there is no difference in the nutritional value, but the taste and appearance of the free-range eggs are certainly more appetising. How many more of these real country treats are to be lost?

Not only were the cultivated fruits of the countryside in great demand fifty years ago. Mushrooms were much sought after and it was not at all unusual to see a large number of people searching the fields for that most edible of fungi. Most farmers did not mind these activities unless there was a suspicion that folk were gathering mushrooms for sale, and then steps were often taken to prevent this trespassing. One favourite method was to have a rather aggressive bull grazing in a field that produced a good crop of mushrooms. This was a great deterrent since even country folk are not too keen to suffer the indignity of being chased by a bull, let alone people from urban areas. The gamekeepers were also against this invasion of the fields, particularly in areas where the woods were well stocked with hand-reared pheasants, and made it their business to turn even local people away when they came too close to their precious charges.

Gathering blackberries was another popular pastime, since many country housewives used to make their own jam and blackberry and apple was one of the favourites. Blackberrying can be a very pleasant pastime during the early autumn when the leaves are changing colour and the sun is shining. Many a peaceful, productive hour was spent by the countrywoman of the past in just such a way.

Today neither of these rural bounties is so plentiful. The mushrooms do not seem to like a lot of the modern fertilisers, but where a field is suitable and has had a dressing of the right chemical, a remarkably large crop is sometimes produced, although it can then be several years before even a small feed can be found on that pasture. It was said by the old-timers that a field grazed by horses always produced good mushrooms year after year, and this was by and large perfectly true. Now, with very few horses around, at least on the farms, the possible mushroom areas are reduced – another once-appreciated country "perk" diminished.

Much the same has happened with the blackberry crop. In the old days, with a number of hedges being left uncut most years on many farms and with blackberry briars abundant, almost without fail a good crop was produced. Today, with the mechanical hedge-cutter, a lot of farms cut all the hedges every year and so few briars produce a crop of fruit. In a way this is a pity, because many people have a freezer these days and they would be glad to preserve this autumn harvest to use later during the winter months. It is rather depressing sometimes to see cars parked on the roadside with their owners searching the hedgerows, trying to fill a plastic bag with berries. In any case, what fruit is gathered must be contaminated with fumes and dust from the passing traffic – not a very appetising prospect.

3

Eaton Estate is at the centre of this book because it is there that I have lived and worked for over fifty years, employed as a gamekeeper. Now a gamekeeper is in a very fortunate position because his duties carry him over the whole of an estate, and during the shooting season he will visit other adjacent and sometimes distant estates. For this reason I have been able to see at first hand the changes not only in the sporting side of life on a large estate, but also in the day-to-day running of such an estate.

Cheshire in general has been very lucky in that few large estates have been broken up on the death of the owner, as has happened so often over the last fifty years or so in other parts of the country. Death duties have been so heavy that the only way to meet them has been the break-up of the property. Very often the whole estate has had to go under the hammer, although sometimes it has been possible to retain the house and maybe the home farm. Many of the tenant farmers have not been in a position to buy their holding and it has been very sad to see these farms changing hands, very often after one family has been tending the land for many generations.

On the other hand some of the tenants have been able to purchase their holdings, probably with the help of a bank loan, and in these days of rocketing rents are in a much sounder position to make farming a viable proposition. In some cases they have even been able to add to the acreage as adjacent farms come on the market. These days many of the pre-war farms of eighty or so acres would need a lot of concentrated husbandry to be profitable, and eight hundred acres seems much nearer the mark.

Vast areas of Cheshire have escaped the break-up of property. Take the south-western corner, where there is Peckforton Estate with its lovely castle situated roughly between Chester and Crewe. Close by is Beeston Castle, now a national monument, steeped in history. Peckforton has been owned by the Tollemache family for centuries and is still run as a family estate, although the present Lord Tollemache does not spend much time there. The shooting is still retained by His Lordship, but on a commercial basis. Peckforton Castle is little used as a residence, but it is a favourite place for the Cheshire Hunt Ball and now and again other social occasions.

Some short distance further south along the Cheshire hills is another castle, Cholmondeley, the residence of the Marquess of Cholmondeley and a well-kept country estate, maintained to a very high standard. Shooting also takes place here, although on a comparatively small scale, and is retained by the Marquess. A great huntsman, the Marquess of Cholmondeley was at one time joint master of the Cheshire Hounds, and foxes are still on the gamekeepers' "banned list" of predators! Prince Charles frequently visits this estate and takes part with his team of horsemen in cross-country events. It is all good hunting country in this part of Cheshire.

Between Peckforton and Cholmondeley and a little to the west lies Bolesworth Castle, the home of the Barbour family. This is another sporting estate and has been retained almost in its entirety. Much of the land is now farmed by the estate, presumably to keep the property intact; maybe for tax or other reasons, "in hand" farming seems to be increasing on large estates. Unfortunately this must mean many less tenant farmers, and maybe overall less efficient farming, but at least

41

it ensures the maintenance of a large property and with it, usually, much better-preserved sporting facilities.

These estates all have castles and, including Beeston Castle, make four ranged along the Cheshire hills. Beeston was obviously built for military purposes in a long-gone era, but the others, Peckforton, Cholmondeley and Bolesworth, appear to be grand stately homes, built to complement the most attractive surroundings of the Cheshire hills. There is a magnificent view from each of these castles: on a clear day a panoramic view of the Welsh mountains, and from many points a distant vista of the Dee and Mersey estuaries. Not quite so attractive, but still very pleasing, is the view of the Cheshire plain seen from these high vantage-points in the hills.

On lower ground between the hills and the river Dee lies a compact and sporting estate, Carden. At Carden, with its rocky outcrops and lake, much good shooting is provided for a syndicate. The estate is administered by trustees of the late Sir John Leche, and here the land is farmed by tenant farmers.

In the last decade or so the husbandry on most of these estates has changed dramatically. At one time most of Cheshire was devoted to dairy farming, but today, although many herds of cows are still maintained, there is also a vast amount of arable land. This arable land produces various crops, but the two main cereals are wheat and barley. A fair amount of Cheshire being between heavy loam and clay, it lends itself well to the growing of wheat, but of course these  cereals are grown according to market demand and very often for feed on the farm itself. Quite a lot of maize is grown in some areas and this crop is silaged, usually in September when the cobs of corn are fully grown. The farming pattern is much changed from fifty years ago, when only the lighter soils were used as arable, but modern machinery and the arrival of such a large variety of fertilisers have made it viable to plough the heavier soils.

Eaton is still more or less the same acreage as it was in the nineteen-twenties, in the days of the second Duke, "Bend-Or". Despite the deaths of the second, third, fourth and fifth Dukes over the past fifty years, it is still run as a large agricultural estate, but many changes, as everywhere else, were brought about by the second world war. The one that probably changed the face of Eaton Estate more than any other was the building of an airfield on the deer park. Although the deer no longer roamed the park in the nineteen-twenties, it was still a most picturesque place, covering approximately a thousand acres, with vast numbers of mature and gnarled oaks. Lines of these oaks stretched to the far distance and made excellent gallops for the horses kept at Eaton, but with the building of the airfield – an emergency landing strip, it was called – about half the park was swallowed up, plus a good acreage of dairy farms.

The second Duke, being a very patriotic and brave man, as his decorations from the first world war showed, did not raise too many objections to this spoiling of his beautiful park until, when planes started to use it, the powers that be wanted to fell a very large and magnificent cedar of Lebanon tree that was on the approach to one of the runways. He was furious about this, and would only agree to a very limited amount being taken out of the top of the tree. This was eventually done, and that tree still stands today.

At the end of the war the land was handed back to Eaton Estate and is now used for agricultural purposes, but the concrete runways are still there, covering a large area of ground. Although wasted as far as farming is concerned, the concrete areas have had their uses. The present Duke, the sixth, at one time owned a small aircraft and naturally used one of the old runways for departing from and arriving at Eaton, but more recently he has taken to a helicopter, which does not need the runway.

For several years the Cheshire Show was held on this old airfield, and the runways were most useful for car parking and as walkways for those attending the show. Unfortunately the access lanes were not suitable to deal with the large amount of traffic bringing visitors to the Show, and eventually this great event in the rural calendar had to be moved and has taken up a permanent site at Tatton Park. Being close to the motorway system and with rather better access, Tatton seems to have revived the fortunes of the Cheshire Show.

Quite a lot of other events have taken place on the old airfield. A cross-country event for four-in-hand coaches started and finished from this venue a number of years ago, and since His Royal Highness Prince Philip was taking part, this naturally created great interest locally in this sport. There is now a permanent point-to-point course on the old airfield which is used in the spring of the year by two different local hunts, Sir Watkin Wynn's Hounds and the Flint and Denbigh. These meetings draw good crowds, but it is a rather exposed area and even in April it can be a pretty cold day out!

The late Duke of Westminster, Robert, the present Duke's father, had quite a lot of forestry work done on this exposed place, planting belts and clumps of softwood and mixed trees. These areas are growing well and in years to come it will look much more like a park again. Will deer ever roam the area? That is anybody's guess!

One end of the old deer park, close to the Hall itself, was for many years a private nine-hole golf course, where Bend-Or would often play a round on his own. At other times there would be a golf tournament with a large house-party,

when the well-known golfing names of the day would be playing. Those were great days, when caddies were supplied from the Estate staff – usually the younger men, for there were no golf trollies and a full bag of clubs was a pretty heavy load even for a young chap. This caddying created an interest in the game and at least two of those old caddies are still playing on that course fifty years on.

Today the golf course has been extended to eighteen holes, taking in part of the park which the airfield didn't, and now that the belts of trees and various other landscaping are maturing rapidly, the scene is a very pleasant one. The club, called Eaton Golf Club, with a large membership and an elegant clubhouse that blends well into the surroundings, has created more jobs in a rural setting, but it is still rather amazing that the present Duke suffers the passage of so many cars past his residence, although they pass some distance away. However, all the members of the Grosvenor family I have known have been fairly tolerant people, and no doubt His Grace is quite happy with the knowledge that a lot of people are enjoying a game of golf in such tranquil surroundings.

Sport of all types played a large part in the life of Bend-Or, the second Duke of Westminster – golf, tennis, racing, hunting and of course shooting. During the nineteen-thirties large tennis house-parties were held at least once or twice during the summer, when once again well-known players of the sport would be present and other members of the house-party would try their skill against them. The game was played much on the lines of the tennis tournaments at Wimbledon. A number of the younger employees on the estate would be in attendance as ball boys and refreshments would be served at the appropriate times by the household staff. In those days there were two tennis courts, one grass and one indoor hard court. Today the grass court is no longer, but the hard court with its huge domed roof is still used by the family and guests.

Bend-Or was always keenly interested in horses and kept a very well-known stud farm, where many famous racehorses were bred. This tradition has been carried on by his widow, Anne, Duchess of Westminster, although, like most things these days, on a much reduced scale. Anne Duchess owned that most famous of racehorses, Arkle, winner of so many races and the Cheltenham Gold Cup in particular.

At one time Bend-Or was very interested in polo and took teams to America. An excellent polo lawn was created close to the Hall, still called the "Polo Ground", and King Alfonso of Spain played there on many occasions. Many ponies were kept for this sport, and a large number of grooms employed to look after them. In his younger days the second Duke was also very keen on hunting and kept a private pack of hounds at Eaton with which to hunt over the vast estate. Woe betide any gamekeeper who didn't have a fox on his beat when the hounds arrived!

He was also very fond of boar-hunting, but not in this country. An estate in France, at Mimazon, provided this for him and several men from Cheshire were employed there. Before the second world war, when the park was intact, there was one corner fenced off with iron railings, about fifteen acres in all. This was always called the "Piggery" and was constructed with the sole purpose of holding wild boar! Even an ornamental brick building had been constructed, which was obviously intended to be a food store. It is pure conjecture, but did Bend-Or have in mind introducing boar-hunting to Cheshire? There are no records to that effect, but he must have had some such idea, for it is hardly likely that the wild boar would be in the Piggery just to look at.

At Aldford there is an area, now part of the home farm, which was in effect a racecourse — a strip of ground about thirty yards wide and covering a distance of one mile in an oval shape. This was obviously used as a training ground for the racehorses and is in fact marked on some maps as such, although always known locally as the racecourse. This was a favourite spot of Bend-Or's, and with one side of the oval running along the river Dee, it certainly is a most attractive place. Even in his declining years he would take a gallop round the racecourse on one of his favourite horses. Maybe two horses would be brought to the mounting block by a groom, then the Duke would arrive by car and take each horse around the course before returning to Eaton. At certain times of the year the gamekeepers were informed of the intended gallops and it was their duty to tour the racecourse and drive any game birds, pheasants or partridges, from the area. The reason was that the sudden eruption of a covey of partridge or a noisy cock pheasant could very easily cause a galloping horse to swerve or shy, possibly with dire circumstances for the rider. After the Duke had departed, Mr Hamilton, the farm manager of those days, was responsible for having the horses' hoof-marks trodden down. A roller could not be used, on orders from His Grace, so a number of men were always detailed for this task. It always had to be done as soon as the Duke had departed, since there was no telling when he would pay another visit!

Over the years many grooms were needed to look after all the horses, and at one time it was said that when the polo ponies and other horses were being exercised, the leading horse was just turning round at the end of Belgrave drive as the last was starting at the top end. This was probably a bit exaggerated – Belgrave drive is a mile and a quarter long!

Almost the last groom employed by Bend-Or was a product of another era, and had worked for the Grosvenor family all his life. "Shadow" Thomas was his name, "Shadow" because of his small and frail stature. Once, whilst having a quiet pint of beer in the Grosvenor Arms at Aldford, he was approached by a stranger who soon bought him another drink and got chatting about Eaton Hall and the Duke. Shadow was very non-committal, replying with a lot of "I couldn't tell you" and "I dare say". It soon became obvious that not much information was to be forthcoming from the ancient servant, and the stranger, who turned out to be a press reporter, was getting rather frustrated. After buying the old lad another drink, he said, "You mean to say you don't know anything and can't tell me anything after working at Eaton for, what did you say, fifty-two years?" Old Shadow, wily customer that he was, replied, "That's right, Mester, that's why I've worked at Eaton fifty-two years." Shadow had had some free beer and the reporter left in disgust, but perhaps in some ways a wiser man.

Shooting has always been of the best quality at Eaton, and the years between the two world wars were probably the heyday of this particular sporting activity, as I have

47

described in my previous book, *Come Dawn, Come Dusk*. It was not at all unusual for close on two thousand pheasants to be killed in one day's shooting, and the Grosvenors have always insisted that all the shooting be the most sporting it is possible to produce. In those halcyon days, up to twenty gamekeepers were employed to rear and protect pheasants and partridges, both of which were reared in large numbers. Many famous people would be at the house-parties held on a shooting week-end, and practically all of them would be good shots and familiar with the etiquette, which was such an important part of a day's shooting. It was an impressive sight to see the guns with their attendant loaders and cartridge carriers proceeding to the numbered pegs from which each guest would shoot. The gamekeepers in their livery of green velvet, white breeches and gold-braided hat, when they appeared out of a wood with the beaters in white smocks and red felt bush-hats, presented an almost feudal scene which, alas, is gone forever now – three gamekeepers, with what can only be described as a motley of beaters, cannot possibly present such an attractive picture as a shooting party did in those far-off days. Admittedly, with modern methods and modern feeds excellent sport can be provided with much less labour than was needed fifty years ago, but the actual cost today ensures that shooting is on a much reduced scale.

Snipe shooting was always very popular with the second Duke, and Eaton has a fairly large area of marshy land which in those days held large numbers of the small elusive bird during the winter months. These withen beds, as they are called, were looked after very carefully to ensure that the snipe would be present when required and also to make sure that the guns could get to a suitable position. Most summers, when the beds were dry, a local farmer was asked to allow his cattle to roam through them and graze some of the succulent growth; this reduced the cover and produced a very suitable feeding ground for the long-billed, long-legged little bird since snipe are unable to insert their bills into the ground to feed if the reeds and grass are too dense.

Butts were also constructed for the guns to hide in, connected by a walkway of planks raised a couple of feet above the ground since quite a lot of water would be in the beds when shooting took place. These planks were nearly all cut from the local poplar trees, a tree which loves wet ground and produces timber which seems to last indefinitely as long as it is under water for part of the year. Some of those planks are still in the withen beds today, although the butts have gone, carried away by flood water.

The snipe were driven over the guns by the gamekeepers and made most elusive targets, but despite this, such was the standard of shooting that His Grace and maybe a couple of guests would kill quite a presentable number. In such boggy ground with many shallow pools, large numbers of wildfowl naturally took advantage of the ideal conditions, but despite the number of these ducks that went over the guns when the keepers were driving the beds and meadows beyond, the Duke and his guests never shot them – it was snipe only.

The marl pits, which I have already described, were an ideal feeding and resting place for both members of the snipe family, the full snipe and jack snipe, which were always present during the autumn and winter fifty years ago. His Grace, when the mood took him, would visit these pits with a couple of keepers in attendance and shoot the zig-zagging little bird as it rose from its watery resting-place. Even when visiting these pits, the Duke always shot with two guns, which entailed Fred Milton, his loader, being in attendance. On approaching the pit one keeper would go to one side, whilst the other with his dog would remain with the Duke and Fred Milton. The detached keeper's job was to make the snipe rise from the pits. By making a very quiet ssh-sshing sound it was possible to make the birds rise singly, or two or three at a time. These little birds really do move and take evasive action when disturbed, but it was not unusual for the Duke to kill a right and a left in quick succession and, changing guns, do the same again! Today, many of these ponds have been filled in, and the snipe have had to find a more suitable habitat.

At one time practically every one of these ponds had at least one pair of nesting reed buntings, that most attractive of buntings with its black head and white collar, locally known as the "pit sparrow". Clinging to a swaying reed and uttering its not too musical attempt at a song, it had a certain attraction

49

that is rarely seen or heard around these pits today. A few do still nest in the withen beds, but it is no longer as widespread as in the past.

In many cases the ponds are badly overgrown, so fewer mallard take advantage of them as nesting sites and other waterfowl are affected as well. Moorhens and coots at one time nested on most pits, and it was a familiar sight in the spring of the year to see the local schoolchildren making for the fields with long poles — sometimes even their mothers' clothes-props were commandeered! The gamekeepers frowned on this activity, as they knew what the long pole was for. The children would tie a large spoon on the end, which enabled them to reach out to the moorhens' and coots' nests and, by gently getting an egg on the spoon, bring it to dry land without getting wet feet! Those eggs were very popular either hard-boiled in a salad or for cake-making purposes. The gamekeepers suspected that the children would also collect duck or even pheasant eggs whilst on these expeditions, so usually chased the children off. Nevertheless, many of the children of those days were pretty crafty and usually managed to get a pocketful of waterfowl eggs before being chased by the keeper. In fact it is doubtful if any of the children would have dared take a game bird or duck egg home; their parents, almost certainly being employed by the estate, would have had something to say about that, knowing full well that if it was suspected that they were encouraging their children to rob the nests of game birds, it could lead to them losing their jobs.

Today, with few exceptions, it is illegal to take any birds' eggs, and a good thing too, but it is doubtful if those birds-nesting and egg-collecting children of the past had any effect on the number of wild birds. There appeared to be very little change in the number of nesting birds until comparatively recently, when such widespread use of chemicals of all kinds, both fertilisers and sprays, became allegedly essential to make husbandry a viable proposition.

Although the gamekeepers chased those birds-nesting children off, they would give them a copper or two when told where there was a pheasant or partridge nest, and the children also benefited by learning quite a lot about nature. They learned that certain herbage meant the possibility of such and such a bird's nest, and with their expeditions into the countryside they saw a lot of other wildlife. Maybe early in the spring they would watch the courtship play of the "mad March hare" or, with luck, one stoat chasing another with the frenzy that is only seen in spring. The appearance of the early hedgerow flowers, primroses, cowslips, campion and, in late April or early May, the white blossom of the hawthorn – all these meant something to those children of the countryside. The arrival of the cuckoo and swallow was noted down in many a child's diary, but today so little notice is taken of these seasonal occurrences of nature that only in later life will it be realised what has been missed. Television and pop music are in the end so artificial, and cannot compare with watching and enjoying nature in all its wondrous changes and glory.

4

Eaton Hall, with its large staff, was always administered independently from the estate itself. There was a secretary who dealt with the running of the myriad items essential to the efficiency of such an establishment. Each section had its head, from the housekeeper down to the head scullery maid, but all requirements went through the secretary's office. The secretary was in effect the kingpin, and a power in the land.

The estate itself was under the control of an estate agent, whose responsibility covered everything outside the bounds of the gardens of the Hall, although he could be concerned within those precincts when occasion demanded it. Major Basil Kerr was the agent during the pre-war period and lived in what was, to all intents and purposes, a stately home within the domain of a stately home. The Paddocks at Eccleston, a village near Chester (four and a half miles from Chester Station, according to the stationery of those days), is still lived in by the present estate agent, Mr R.M.C. Jones, but under rather different conditions from those which existed before the war. Major Kerr was provided with a gardener and chauffeur as well as a cook and household staff – in fact he lived very much like a gentleman of those days. A gentleman he was, being loved and respected by all the employees on Eaton Estate. The office which dealt with the overall running of the vast acres was next to The Paddocks, but compared with the number of people required in the present estate office, the staff was meagre. Teddy Wells was the chief clerk, assisted by another clerk and a typist, and these people dealt with all estate affairs. Three of the departments also had an office, in each case with one clerk: the forestry department, with its staff of around eighty woodmen and various odd-job men, the clerk of works' department and the home farm.

These departments still exist, though employing many fewer men, and all departments are now controlled from a central office, which is in fact the converted laundry – yes, there used to be a private laundry on the estate! There is certainly a much larger staff in the office today, but in fairness, the agent is responsible for all of the Grosvenor Estates' agriculture property, which is scattered throughout the land. The present Duke's private secretary has an office there, as indeed does the Duke himself, from where he deals with his many duties as Chairman of Grosvenor Estates. Grosvenor Estates is a trust set up by the second Duke in 1953 to ensure that future Dukes should be able to retain the properties as a whole, and of course be financially sound. Gerald, the present Duke, travels many thousands of miles a year, almost all on Estates business. Many local charitable concerns have persuaded him to become President or Patron and rarely does he miss an important meeting connected with these charities, often travelling up from London just to be present. Although such a busy young man, he is like all the recent Grosvenors in that he always has time to stop and have a few words with his employees, and seems to have his finger on the pulse of all that goes on on the estate.

It was necessary for the forestry department to have its own office in the nineteen-thirties because it controlled such a large number of employees. "Sandy" Myles was the head forester, with the responsibility of maintaining the woodlands on the estate, supplying staff for the private railway and the nine-hole golf course and men to ensure all watercourses were in good condition ("brookers", they were called) and, last but not least as far as the Duke was concerned, looking after the churchyard at Eccleston, the family church.

Forestry was not really practised as a viable proposition. Bend-Or being so keen on shooting, the woods had to be planned and maintained with that in mind, which was not always the best thing for timber production. Large areas of shrubs had to be kept in a suitable condition as flushing points for pheasants, and mature timber, which normally would have been felled and replanted, had to be left for the game birds to roost in. Sandy did not have a particularly easy job, for he also had to fell enough timber to supply the estate sawmill, where numerous items were produced for use on the estate. Some of these, such as field gates, hunting hatches, garden wickets, fencing posts, stakes and rails, can still be seen on the estate today, over fifty years after they came from the sawmill. Modern products of this nature seem to have a very short life by comparison, and the most obvious reason is the way the timber is treated today. Trees are cut down when they are in full leaf, in fact during any month in the twelve; they are then kiln-dried and the wood could easily be used for fencing within a month or two of the tree being felled. Judging by the life-span of the end product, this hardly seems like progress. Also, much damage must be caused to wildlife by felling trees when they are in leaf. Nesting birds in the ground cover must lose their eggs, and no doubt often their fledglings, when the tree crashes to the ground and mechanical implements move in. There must be a reason for this change in the production of our home-grown timber. Is it because a drying kiln has to work all year round to be viable? Or because tree-fellers have become contractors and now travel over a large area all the year to obtain work?

The older methods of dealing with timber were no doubt slower, but there was a lot to be said for them. After being felled during the winter months, and certainly not after February, the tree was taken to the sawmill by horse and timber-carriage, where it was stored with the rest of the season's "crop". By simply pulling a lever, the modern crane-driver can lift a tree butt and place it within an inch of where he wants it, but the way those old waggoners loaded the timber-wagon was something to behold. There were two methods of loading the trees, and often there would be three or four on one load. One method was by using a "three-legs" as they called it. This was a tripod under which the trunk of the tree was drawn by horses, then it was lifted off the ground by use of pulleys, the timber-wagon was backed under it and the tree lowered to a suitable position. This operation was repeated until the wagon had a full load. The other way was to draw all the timber to one spot and, by the clever use of strong ropes and knowledgeable horses, roll the trunks onto the wagon. This appears to be a simple operation, but much skill was needed to get a load that was balanced and safe to take on a road.

All these trees had of course been "dropped" by hand, with no mechanical aids of any sort. The tree-fellers, whose tools were always sharp, would first of all trim all the spurs at the base of the tree with deft strokes of their axes. A "face" would then be cut in one side of the trunk, that is a wedge-shaped piece taken out with the axe at a height of maybe two feet from the base. This face ensured that the tree would fall in the direction required. The trunk itself was then attacked with a cross-cut saw, which required two men to operate, and when two experts were doing this, it appeared to be effortless. The secret, it seems, was never to push the saw, only pull it, and two good men could have a large tree down in no time at all. Sandy Myles being a first-class forester, he insisted that all trees were cut at ground level, and that once a tree was down, all rubbish, small branches and chips of wood had to be burnt, so that in a very short time there was little evidence that a tree ever stood there.

The trees taken to the sawmill during the course of one winter were not touched until the following winter, when they were cut lengthways into planks, two to four inches thick. This operation took place after the trunk of the tree had been cut into pieces around twelve feet long, the normal length of a rail. Once "slabbed", as they called it, the planks were stacked in piles, with pieces of wood between each slab to allow the air to circulate. These piles of slabs were then left until the following winter before being used, so it was

55

two years from the time the tree was felled before the well-seasoned timber was put to use. Most of the timber was also "pickled", that is passed through a large tank containing creosote, which helped to ensure a long life, no matter what purpose it was used for.

The tenant farmers only had to send a horse and lorry to the sawmill at Belgrave, and they were supplied with as much fencing material as they wanted. There was just one condition: Sandy Myles inspected the job the timber was used for, and woe betide any farmer who hadn't made a good job! It was not unknown for Sandy to make them pull the whole lot up and do the job again, maybe only because the fence wasn't straight or the top level! Today, barbed wire is in bigger demand than timber fencing — it is unsightly, dangerous stuff, but once again the price of material and labour has brought about its widespread use.

Tree planting was usually done in October and November, when, as Sandy Myles used to say, "You can tell 'em to grow", whereas if you left it until the spring you had to "ask 'em to grow". Normally more young trees were planted than the number felled, to allow for the inevitable losses. A number of new woods were planted, not so much for timber but more for game woods. Today they are mature stands of timber and still used for the purpose for which they were planted, pheasant shooting. No longer is home-grown timber processed for local use, though, and Sandy Myles' headquarters at the Belgrave sawmills ceased to function soon after the war. Now it is one of the best garden centres in the country, covering a very large area with everything available from seeds to camping equipment, mowing-machines and sheds, light refreshments available and a play area for the children.

The forestry department had many fringe jobs which were really estate maintenance, so the woodmen worked in gangs. On such a large estate this was an ideal arrangement, as the men normally worked in the area in which they lived. There was the Overleigh gang, the Bretton gang, the Aldford gang, the Pulford gang and the Park gang. At certain times all the men would be together in one large gang: haymaking was one such time, when the grass in various parts of the park and on the drive-sides was mown and made into hay to be used as feed for the forestry department horses. This haymaking was followed by hedge-cutting, which was usually done on a piece-work basis – they had to work hard to make another couple of bob on their wages! "Faggoting" was a task usually carried out by individual gangs. Faggots were bundles of thinnish undergrowth cut into lengths of about three feet and tied with bands made from withens, the young growth of the willow. Several hundred of these faggots had to be made each year and carted to the "stick house" at the Hall. At the stick house a man was employed full-time chopping these faggots into suitable sizes for lighting fires, and storing them for some time to ensure they would burn well and get a fire going quickly.

During the winter months and when the water level made it possible, the willow wands were harvested from a marshy piece of ground at Aldford called the withen beds, and sold for basket-making. Most of these withens went to Bangor-on-Dee, a village higher up the Dee, where baskets are still made to this day – not from Aldford withens, though.

The forestry department had one more regular job during the summer months. The estate had seven main drives giving access to public roads, with a lodge at each exit. Every Saturday morning from spring to autumn, the lawns to these lodges had to be mown – not with a mowing-machine, but by hand with a scythe. Those old foresters could really use a scythe and would make as good a job of the lawns as many a modern mowing-machine. The art was in the sharpening of the blade and the way it was swung: not too much and not too little. There are very few people about today who could sharpen the blade, let alone mow a lawn with it.

The drives themselves were also maintained to a very high standard, and it was the custom for the older forestry men to be allocated to looking after the drives – no retiring at sixty-five then. The sides were regularly edged, the leaves brushed up and any shrubs or bushes trimmed back. One old lad, who was responsible for the Aldford approach drive, had lots of bushes – privet, laurel and so on – that needed regular trimming. Ellis Thomas was his name, and what a craftsman he was! Using a short-handled brushing hook, he kept the growth in check and it was practically impossible to see any cuts he had made. Once again, half the secret was keeping the tool sharp, and Ellis used a quite small piece of slate for this purpose. Sharpening the hook was actually one of Ellis's biggest jobs; he would stand for hours, surveying his handiwork and rubbing the blade gently with the piece of slate. It also gave him plenty of time for a smoke! The old men enjoyed these maintenance jobs, which no doubt gave them the feeling of still being wanted and useful.

Many main watercourses run through the estate, and all of these were under the care of Sandy Myles. Drainage was most important, especially as the Eaton part of Cheshire is mostly very heavy clay. There were no mechanical means of pipe-laying, ditching or brook clearance, and all the work had to be done by hand. The farmers normally attended to the drains and ditches on their holding at the "back end" of the year, as described in Chapter 1, but unless the main watercourses were also running freely, the farmers' work had achieved little. Three of Sandy's men had the task of ensuring a free flow of water through to the river Dee, and a dirty, wet job it was. There were no rubber boots in those days, but they did have longer versions of the old-style fireman's leather jack-boot. These leather thigh-boots kept out most of the water, but as the day wore on, the leather naturally soaked up more and more water despite being dressed with neat's foot oil (a thin penetrating oil, usually obtainable at tripe shops and made great use of by country people for waterproofing purposes, not always with the greatest of success). By night the boots had reached such a state that it was almost impossible to walk in them, yet these men were a happy band who took great pride in their work and rarely complained about the conditions under which they laboured. When rubber boots became available they changed working conditions dramatically not only for these "brookers", but also for the vast majority of men who worked on the land and had to be out in all weathers.

In those pre-war days, all the watercourses were carrying good clean water into the Dee. Some of the larger brooks even had the odd trout in them, and trout just cannot exist unless the water is pure and preferably running. Many had watercress in abundance and all of them were the routes taken by eels on their way to the marl pits. During the summer it was not at all uncommon, mostly in the early morning when there was a heavy dew, to see quite large eels wriggling their way across a field and uncannily heading for one of these pits. Eels were always plentiful in those days and at certain times of the year the locals would go "eel bobbing" in the main brook in Aldford. This eel bobbing usually took place when there was a threat of thunder, when for some reason eels were always on the move and ravenous. The old hands scorned the use of rod and line, but by dangling a length of wool, onto which worms had been threaded, from a length of stick into the water, they would simply jerk the eel out onto the bank as soon as it tugged at a worm. The eel's teeth would get enmeshed in the wool and before the luckless fish could free itself, it was out on dry land. There were refinements to this method: the angler would have an umbrella handy and, when an eel took the bait, it would find itself stranded in an upturned brolly. Maybe the umbrella was taken originally in case the thunderstorm broke!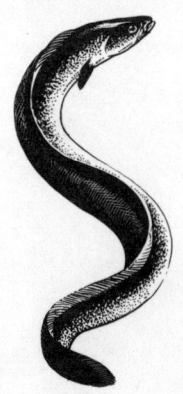

A mill that once ground the grain for the local farmers was situated on this same Aldford brook. A descendant of the last miller told me that around the turn of the century, when the mill was flourishing, there was an eel trap installed and literally hundredweights of fish were caught. Apparently these eels were packed in barrels, still alive, and finished up as jellied eel in the Lancashire cotton towns.

Today the watercourses no longer get the loving care of those three old brookers, who, incidentally, all lived to be between eighty and ninety years old. As the years went by, the main streams were taken over by the Dee and Clwyd Water Authority, which left only the woodland ditches for the brookers to attend to, and as these old lads retired or died they were not replaced. Now there has been another change and water is the responsibility of the North West Water Authority, whose main task in this rural area is to try to ensure that all water going into the Dee is not polluted. Now and again a mechanical ditcher will do the ditches out, and a drag-line dredger the main brooks. The field drains get little attention, the land being "mole drained" as and when it is considered necessary. Most of the main watercourses are now so badly polluted with chemicals, fertilisers, sprays and farmyard effluent that no longer do eels wend their way to the pits or watercress flourish. It is doubtful whether those men of long ago would have lived to such a ripe old age if they had had to work in the stinking mire that fills the ditches today.

It will be seen that the men of the forestry department had so many and varied tasks to perform that quite a number of them were not in the true sense woodmen. It would need a vivid imagination indeed to visualise the staff that handled the narrow-gauge railway as woodmen. This railway served many purposes on the estate and came under the control of that man of many parts, Sandy Myles. An engine driver and a guard were employed to run the railway, with staff available to help with loading and unloading as required. The permanent way extended from the "stick house" at the Hall to a main line (Great Western) siding at Balderton, a small hamlet on the estate. There was also a branch line to the sawmill at Belgrave, with another line on to the clerk of works' yard at Cuckoo's Nest. The total length of line must have been around four miles. It ran either through or alongside woodlands, and when the engine appeared through a sylvan glade, pulling maybe four trucks laden with coal, it presented a fairyland sight. The Hall needed vast quantities of coal to maintain even a reasonable degree of warmth during the winter months, and the train delivered it. The normal trains brought ten or twelve trucks at a time to the Balderton sidings, where the Eaton Railway would pick up its load and head for the Hall. Many other items of merchandise were also collected from the Balderton sidings for delivery to either the sawmill or the builders' yard. Peat was one item that was required each year in the gardens to lighten the heavy Cheshire soil. Up to one hundred tons would arrive, which had to be transported to Eaton.

There were passenger coaches as well as goods wagons, and although these coaches were not used as much as the wagons, they were called into service when the second Duke was holding a shooting party. It was usually after lunch that the train appeared with its load of shooting gentlemen, and also on board would be the ladies, who only put in an appearance after lunch. The train would wait until the first drive of pheasants was over, and then take most of the ladies back to the Hall. The children on the estate quite naturally loved to have a ride on this narrow-gauge railway, but were not normally allowed to do so. However, on special occasions such as Royal events there would be a fête in the park and that was when the children got their rides. The engine driver must have been weary of travelling back and to over the same piece of track, for many trips were needed before the children tired of the experience.

In due course the steam engine was replaced by a diesel unit, which could haul a fair load more than a steam engine could. There were proper engine sheds at the Belgrave sawmill, where the rolling stock was serviced and maintained, but the lines needed little in the way of maintenance and this was usually carried out by the driver and guard – they couldn't have been in a trade union! At the end of the second world war the railway system on the estate was discontinued and the engines and rolling stock disposed of, but some of it is still doing service on the Romney, Hythe and Dymchurch Light Railway. The present Duke, Gerald (the sixth), who is very keen on preserving anything to do with the history of the Grosvenors, has managed to get back one or two of the passenger coaches of this private railway and is having them restored. The permanent way has long since been pulled up, so there is very little chance of seeing them running at Eaton again.

Estate property was and has always been kept in very good repair, and this is the main function of the clerk of works' department. Before the war a number of tradesmen were employed to cover all jobs liable to crop up on a large estate, from joiners right through to plasterers and plumbers, but no electricians, except for one at the Hall, as there was no electricity on the estate until pretty well into the nineteen-thirties. These men were all employed on repair work, as no actual building took place on the estate until much later, well after the second Duke's death. The painters were always busy: with so many houses and farms on the estate, the good weather was fully taken up with outside painting, since it was the policy to paint the exteriors of all estate buildings at least once every five years.

There is a much smaller staff on the clerk of works' books now, and the yard is in the village of Aldford, making use of what used to be the old gasworks. Many years ago, gas from these works was supplied to most of the cottages at Aldford. The coming of electricity caused the closing down of the gas-making plant, but some of the cottages still have the gas pipes visible. There was also a gas-making plant at Eaton which supplied the Hall and cottages in the vicinity. These works were sited some distance from the Hall, close to the river Dee, and after being closed, were used to store defunct horse-drawn vehicles of all kinds.

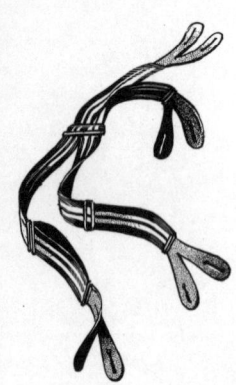

The clerk of works' yard at Aldford is on a smaller scale than the old one at Cuckoo's Nest and employs few craftsmen like old Billy Maddocks, one of the estate joiners. Billy was a top-class tradesman who worked on the estate most of his life, but as he got older, he got more forgetful. All the employees on the estate were allowed to have a day off to go to the races during Chester race week and on one such occasion, Billy rushed home for lunch and to get changed before cycling into Chester. He went upstairs after a hurried lunch, but there was soon a lot of shouting and cursing to be heard – he couldn't find his braces! Giving it up, he came downstairs with his clean shirt and trousers on but nothing to hold the trousers up, demanding that his wife find some string to tie up the trousers and swearing she had hidden the braces to stop him going to the races. Eventually Billy got to the races, but when he got back home, his wife had still not found his braces. All was revealed at bedtime: in his haste to get changed, he had put his clean shirt on over his braces, which he had left over his shoulders when he changed his trousers!

The clerk of works' department always sent joiners all over the estate, usually just before the start of the hunting season, to see that the hunting hatches were in working order. Hunting hatches are small wicket gates just large enough for a horse to pass through and are situated between farms, or give onto lanes or woods. Many of them were locked out of the hunting season, but all had to work satisfactorily at other times, swinging shut after a horse and rider had passed through. Billy Maddocks and his labourer were working on one such gate which needed a fair amount of planing to get it to work and, wanting to check up on progress, Billy asked his labourer for his two-foot rule. The labourer couldn't find it in the joiner's "bass" and told Billy so. Both hunted high and low without luck until Bill started to scratch around in the shavings. John, his labourer, suddenly noticed that Billy was using the two-foot rule to move the shavings with. When he told Billy so, there was hell to pay, with John getting the blame!

With Eaton Hall, its private chapel and stables covering such a vast area, some provision had to be made in case of fire. Before the days of the internal combustion engine, should there have been a fire at the Hall, a horse-drawn appliance would have had to come the four miles or so from Chester, leaving little chance of stopping a small fire growing into a large one. For many years, therefore, the Hall had its own fire brigade. Members of the staff at the Hall were taught to man the fire-fighting equipment and had periodic training sessions under their fire chief. They were all supplied with a uniform which was worn at these training sessions, but it is doubtful if there would have been time for the part-time firemen to change into their kit had the fire appliance been called out to a real fire. A bell over the fire station was the means of calling the men in case of an emergency, but not only were the trained men supposed to attend; all estate employees who heard the warning also had to rush to the Hall. Sometimes the bell would be rung for a practice session, just to see the response of outside staff. With so many gardeners and estate employees there was usually a very large crowd assembled.

When fire engines were motorised and a fully equipped appliance could get to Eaton in a matter of minutes, there was no need for an engine at the Hall, but well into the nineteen-thirties it was still in its shed and maintained by the remaining staff who had been firemen. No doubt it would still have been in serviceable condition, but as far as I know there was never a serious fire in the Gothic Eaton Hall, so the capabilities of the machine were not really tested. Better to be prepared, though, than to have to stand and watch a small fire develop into a large one: Carden Hall, only a few miles from Eaton, was completely gutted by fire before any help could reach it and has never been rebuilt. Maybe an on-site appliance such as the one at Eaton would have prevented that disaster way back in the early part of the century.

5

With so many employees on a large estate in pre-war days, there was naturally always plenty of activity and the big house, in this case Eaton Hall, would be the centre of it. The Hall was always a hum of activity, even though the second Duke of Westminster was a great traveller and was often away for quite long periods. Bend-Or was always a restless man, seldom in one place for long, but with his great wealth (his income in the early nineteen-thirties was reputed to be a pound a minute), there was very little that wasn't possible to him. Travel was not so easy in those days, and although passenger flying was in its early days, Bend-Or was never known to take to the air. Today the present Duke, the sixth, has his own helicopter and makes it his main means of getting from place to place quickly. Trains, although not quite so swift as the modern Inter-City service, were at least nearly always on time and, for those travelling first-class, a most comfortable means of transport. His Grace was frequently travelling between Chester and London and would usually be taken to Crewe by car, thus avoiding the irksome task of having to change trains. In those days only a few trains were through trains, and those were usually Holyhead to Euston – in fact the Irish boat trains. Being crowded, they did not meet with the Duke's likes; one thing he detested was being in a crowd, so it was to Crewe by car, and a comfortable journey.

He was in a way a rather solitary man and hated strange faces – so much in fact, that it was said he rarely spoke to a new servant for at least a year – so to be called by your Christian name was indeed a great honour which few achieved. "Benny", as his friends called him, travelled a great deal on the Continent, mainly in France and on the French Riviera in particular. Having two large yachts, the *Flying Cloud* and the *Cutty Sark*, enabled him to entertain his friends almost anywhere without being in public places. Frequently, one yacht would be in the south of France and the other somewhere in English waters. The *Flying Cloud* was actually a replica of the tea clipper of that name and provided the Duke with leisurely cruises on the warm waters of the Mediterranean, often visiting the Greek islands.

My father was chief steward on the *Flying Cloud* (Mr Warder was chief on the *Cutty Sark*, although often they would both be on the same yacht!) and on one occasion the schooner was tied up at Genoa awaiting orders. The *Cutty Sark* had taken His Grace from Deauville on the French coast of the English Channel to Loch Laxford on the Duke's estate in Sutherland, North Scotland. A cablegram arrived on the *Flying Cloud* with instructions for my father to be on the *Cutty Sark* at a given time two days hence. This meant one mad dash to catch a train and proceed overland as quickly as possible to be in Scotland by the appointed time. By sheer luck the train connections were good and the time given for arrival was just made. Once aboard the *Cutty Sark*, my father discovered that there was to be a dinner party that night for fourteen people, which duly took place. As soon as the dinner was finished the Duke turned to my father and thanked him for coming from Italy, saying, "Make your way back, Mursell, I'll be joining the *Flying Cloud* in a day or two." An overland and no doubt very trying journey from Italy to Scotland to help serve one dinner to fourteen people – could that happen today?

The *Cutty Sark*, although fitted out as a luxurious yacht, had been completed shortly after the end of the first world war as a fast torpedo-boat destroyer. The Duke was very fond of this ship – being speedy, it could get him about pretty fast if the occasion arose. During the Spanish Civil War, Bend-Or for some reason known only to himself wanted to see what was happening in Spain, so the *Cutty Sark* had to cruise down the Spanish coast quite close to the shore. Shelling was observed, and the Duke gave orders to get closer so he could see what was taking place. The Captain (Capt. Mack) naturally carried out orders, but had hardly done so before the guns were turned on the *Cutty Sark*. Fortunately the Spaniards must have been ill-trained gunners and failed to score a hit, and with the speed of the yacht she was soon out of range. Further down the coast the yacht was several miles offshore when plumes of water appeared ahead.

These were obviously warning shots across her bow and a hasty retreat was indicated. At some spot along the Spanish coast His Grace was put ashore, and when he returned aboard, course was immediately set for England and the river Mersey. No-one ever knew the real reason for this trip, but it was noted that on the night of his arrival back at Eaton, the only guest at the Duke's dinner table was Mr Winston Churchill, later of course to become Sir Winston. Anyone can hazard a guess at this coincidence, but the two men had always been good friends. Was it a fact-finding operation?

Another trip of the *Cutty Sark* took place during the Abyssinian War. The yacht was lying at a port in the south of France when numerous packing-cases were brought alongside. These were taken aboard, and shortly afterwards the Duke arrived. A short cruise was taken and then out of the blue the Captain was ordered to make course for the Red Sea! In due course she tied up in an Abyssinian port, the cases were unshipped and put on a train for Addis Ababa, and to the surprise of the ship's company the Duke travelled with them. It was understood that the cases contained medical supplies. No doubt they did, but feeling had it that that was a good cover for the Duke to enter the war-torn country. Once again, was it an unofficial fact-finding mission? Who knows, or ever will.

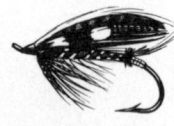

Bend-Or made frequent trips to Monte Carlo, Cannes and many French resorts as well as visits to his Scottish estates and, for the salmon fishing, to the land of the midnight sun, way up in the Arctic circle at Bosskop, Norway. Nevertheless, the numerous staff at Eaton did not have an easy time, for very often if the Duke was not in residence, one of his friends would be staying for a day or two, and anyway he was quite likely to turn up at very short notice indeed; sometimes, in fact, the train might have left London before the staff at Eaton knew of the Duke's impending arrival!

Eaton Hall, the one of the nineteen-thirties (since demolished and re-built in the modern style), was a large, rambling Gothic building, very impressive when viewed from the well-known Golden Gates, but it must have been hard work for the staff to maintain in a condition befitting a Duke with many rooms and long corridors. In fact, the kitchen was so far from the dining room than when a dinner party was in progress, lads from the outside departments were brought in to "run the dinner". They had to dash down the corridors with the food-laden trolleys to ensure that the meal was hot when it reached the dining table. This running the dinner was a coveted job; although it was often late at night when the task was finished and the pay a pittance, the chef usually found some left-over food for the lads to take home! Such food was a real treat, often of a kind well beyond the means of the estate workers of those days.

There were coal fires in practically every room, and it is hard to imagine the amount of work involved in cleaning the grates out, let alone lighting the fires and keeping them stoked up. There was a lift which took the fuel to the various floors, but it still left a lot of humping to be done! The amount of coal used was colossal.

All the staff employed at the hall were fed, and there were so many that it needed staff to look after staff! Even large houses today rely on daily workers, having to run on a restricted budget, and the same applies at the modern Eaton Hall. Gone are the days of large staff with their liveries, footmen in their resplendent dress are no longer in evidence, and only the butler maintains those pre-war standards of elegance. In the second Duke's day several chauffeurs were employed, and when a large number of guests were due to arrive at Chester or Crewe stations a local taxi firm would have two or three cars based at Eaton, ready to be called upon day or night. This must have been a very welcome source of income for the Chester taxis, with the meter ticking away for twenty-four hours at a time.

I recall one incident in which a taxi was concerned. For once the second Duke was spending Christmas at Eaton, and there was quite a house-party in residence. A two-day shoot had taken place on the twenty-second and twenty-third of December, and most of the guests were stopping over the festive season. The gamekeepers had the almost impossible task of disposing of over two thousand pheasants which had been shot. The gift list was a long one and to ensure that the larder was cleared before Christmas, an estate lorry was called into service and a taxi was allocated to the game department to deal with the distribution of the birds. I was appointed to go with the taxi and take a brace of pheasants here, a brace of pheasants there. A large number had to be distributed in Chester itself and a taxi-driver was the right man to find his way about the city.

It was mid-morning on the twenty-fourth before the lists were sorted out and the pheasants labelled, so after a quick coffee in the servants' hall, a start was made on the tour of Chester. Christmas Eve has always been a busy time in any town or city, and Chester is no exception. There were pheasants for the Bishop of Chester, the Mayor, the Chief Constable and other senior officers, the manager of the Grosvenor Hotel, the stationmaster and even one particular ticket-collector, and many other fortunate folk. With the heavy traffic, and even in those days some parking problems, it was early afternoon when the task was completed.

On arriving back at Eaton, the taxi was met by Fred Milton, the head gamekeeper, who had another load ready and labelled, and these birds were to be delivered to various people over a large area of Cheshire! It was rather late for lunch, but a snack was soon rustled up by the kitchen staff before the taxi once more set off on its rounds. Although there weren't as many brace of pheasants in this load, the distance to be covered was much greater, so care had to be taken over the route to ensure that we did not retrace our steps. After travelling many miles and making many enquiries for directions on the largely unfamiliar territory, I finally delivered the last brace of pheasants in Crewe, some twenty-odd miles from Chester. At this point, Arthur the taxi-driver suddenly remembered that he hadn't collected his own Christmas dinner, a large joint of pork, which had been ordered from a butcher's in Chester! Back we went to Chester, and fortunately shops didn't close at five o'clock in those days, so the pork was still on the menu for Arthur's Christmas dinner. Arthur decided to call at home with the meat, in case his wife was getting anxious about its and his whereabouts, before taking me back to Eaton. It was by now seven o'clock in the evening, so a cup of tea and piece of cake provided by "Mrs Arthur" were most welcome. Thinking the day's work was completed, we took our refreshment at leisure. Hard luck – it was not so! On our arrival back at Eaton, who should immediately appear but Albert Hopkins, the Duke's valet. "I'm sorry," he said, "but here are some Christmas cards. His Grace wants them delivering at once. I'm afraid you're the only transport free. Will you see to it?"

Of course there wasn't any option really, but on examining the wad of cards I discovered that a large part of the area covered that afternoon had to be travelled again! Petrol in the tank of the taxi was getting low, so the first stop was Arthur's depot to refill – no all-night filling stations in those days.

Then off we went on the postman's run, till by about eleven-thirty that evening only one card was left, for the district nurse in the village of Tattenhall. Fortunately the first person we asked knew the nurse's residence, so a tired Arthur said, "Thank God. Let's get back to Eaton." Albert the valet was still up when we got back – a good many of the staff did not dare go to bed until the Duke did, and Albert was no exception. He was very pleased that the Christmas cards had all been delivered, since the Duke had asked several times during the evening about them. A good stiff whisky was now in order, and as Arthur was about to depart, he was given a bottle of the "mountain dew", with the compliments of His Grace.

This was a most unusual incident, for Bend-Or seldom put pen to paper, let alone sent out Christmas cards, but on this occasion although the envelopes were typed, the cards bore the Duke's signature. Some of those cards could still be treasured by families somewhere in Cheshire.

Bend-Or had great feeling for his employees, especially the older ones. At Christmas time there were always some gifts from Eaton for the old loyal servants – a pudding, perhaps, or mince pies – and the widows in particular were treated very well, usually receiving a blanket at Christmas time. This tradition is very largely kept up today: Gerald, the present and sixth Duke, gives all employees a bottle of whisky, while the estate pensioners receive a cash gift and all past and present employees receive a load of logs. These gifts are not of quite the same importance as they were many years ago, but all the same they are much appreciated by the recipients.

Normally it is the custom at a large country residence like Eaton for the lady of the house to take an interest in the gardens and to be responsible for the overall appearance. This did happen at Eaton, but with a comparatively short time of each year being spent in residence, most of the changes which took place were at the instigation of the head gardener, at that time a Mr Barnes. Bend-Or was keen that all was kept in good order but did little to interfere with the general running of the ninety acres in Mr Barnes' charge. On the Duke's instructions a long and wide border had to contain nothing but blue flowers, and the variety was enormous. In fact there was something in bloom almost the year round, but no bedding plants – that was one thing the Duke was not keen on – and everything had to look as natural as possible. The gardens had originally been landscaped by Capability Brown, so very little was done to alter the work of such an outstanding craftsman. With the land falling in a gentle slope down to the river Dee, the terraces were a wonderful sight viewed from the lake which lies between the gardens and the river. In early summer when the azaleas and rhododendrons are in full bloom the view from the house and terraces is magnificent; on a bright, calm day the colour of the shrubs is often reflected in the lake, giving the impression of one sea of white, yellow and blue.

For many years, partly due to the second world war, and later because several Dukes died over a short span of time, the gardens were not maintained in their pre-war glory. The vast area of greenhouses which had been in use became rather dilapidated and were eventually disposed of. No longer was one gardener employed solely to look after the orchid house, a flower which was a great favourite with Bend-Or, and the boiler which supplied heat to the many greenhouses no longer functioned. All these houses were needed to keep a constant supply of pot plants and cut flowers to decorate the Hall; even though he was likely to arrive at short notice, the Duke expected to see a good show of blooms in many of the rooms.

There were also vegetables to be grown, which had to be of tip-top quality and much earlier than those obtainable elsewhere. A lot of these were grown at Eaton, along with fruit such as peaches and grapes, but the main vegetable garden was some distance away at Aldford, where up to fourteen gardeners were employed; with row upon row of peas, beans, cabbages, carrots and so on, it was more like a market garden than a private one. Fruit – apples, pears and plums – was also grown at Alford, and the foreman gardener there once told me that there were so many varieties of pears that the late ones were only just over before the early ones were ripe! One greenhouse in the Aldford kitchen gardens was built especially for fruit-growing, a sunken house where very early fruit was produced. It contained mainly apple trees in pots which had been grown and treated to produce fruit much earlier than could be done in the normal way, often being in bloom before the trees in the orchard showed any signs of growth. These pot trees had a comparatively short life, and when their usefulness in the "orchard house", as it was called, came to an end, they usually ended up in a cottager's garden. Some are still producing fruit. No-one can name the variety, but that doesn't matter so long as the apples are good.

It is remarkable that so much money, time and labour should have been spent in producing early crops like that, but to Bend-Or home-produced fruit and vegetables seemed to taste so much better, and fifty years ago, there were not the facilities to keep perishable goods very long. Even the ice that was used in the Hall came in huge blocks from Chester, from the Chester Frozen Store, and without a doubt the bulk of it had thawed before it could be used.

It would not be a viable proposition today to have the sort of operation that has been described. With a gardener's wages at, say, eighty pounds a week, the cost of one man would buy a lot of vegetables and fruit in a year, so the kitchen gardens at Aldford no longer exist as such; with over an acre being surrounded by walls twelve feet high, it has proved an ideal spot to rear game by modern methods, since it is well sheltered and practically predator-proof. What was originally used as a store-house and "bothy" is ideal for keeping game-bird eggs prior to hatching in incubators.

The walls and bothy were originally built in 1896, and on one shelf in the bothy can still be seen items of interest recorded by the gardeners of that time: "John Thomas died January the sixth, nineteen hundred and two, buried in Aldford Churchyard". "Cuckoo, April 12th" – did that summer visitor to our country come earlier in those days, or was that particular year blessed with a very early spring? "Chiff-chaff seen in gooseberry bushes, March 14th, 1910", and many more notes of this nature, which show how observant those gardeners of long ago were. Perhaps a lot of the modern gardeners would not know a chiff-chaff if they heard one, let alone saw one! Also noted on the shelves in the bothy

and still to be seen are the dates at which various seeds were sown and crops harvested, a most interesting record of a bygone age.

The second world war put an end to this type of garden, but throughout the war period the emphasis turned to vegetable production. As some of the gardeners joined the armed forces, a number of local women were taken on in their place. These ladies gave a valuable service, being equally as good as men at many of the garden tasks, and most of them eventually joined the Women's Land Army. After the war things were never the same in the gardens either at Eaton or at Aldford. Many of the fruit trees in the kitchen gardens had been taken out to make way for increased vegetable production during the war, and eventually the walled part was taken over by the game department, whilst the remainder was used as a nursery by the forestry department.

At one stage, Sally Duchess took a great interest in the grounds, although she lived at Saighton Grange with "Gerald Duke" and had magnificent gardens there. Quite a bit of tree and shrub planting took place on her instructions, but really it was only replacing the losses over a number of years, and with such a small staff of gardeners nothing ambitious could be done. Today, though, with the sixth Duke and his Duchess living at Eaton for a large part of the year, much has been done to restore the gardens and pleasure grounds to their former glory. Ken Ledward, the present head gardener, has on instructions from the Duchess transformed many aspects of the ninety acres for which he is responsible. Old and worn-out shrubs have been removed and young modern varieties put in their place, a good omen for the future. Much use is also made of summer bedding plants, something only seen to a limited degree at Eaton before. With a larger staff than there has been for a long while, Ken Ledward has achieved much over the last few years, and as time passes and his labours come to fruition, the gardens will without doubt be back to their former glory.

As happens at most stately homes, the gardens at Eaton have always been open to the public on a number of days during the summer, with the takings going to various charities. Easter is the first opening date, when large crowds flock to see the vast areas of golden daffodils swaying in the spring breeze. The large patches of yellow blooms with a backcloth of shrubs in so many varied shades of green are a herald of the summer to come. One year, spring was late in coming, and as the open day approached there was no sign of a yellow bloom, hardly a bud in fact, and all concerned were getting rather anxious. At that time the Duke, the fifth in fact, spent quite a lot of time at his other home, Eley Lodge in Inniskillen. His step-brother, Major Hamilton Stubber, also lived in Ireland and the Duke must have been talking to him about the lateness of the daffodils at Eaton. Arriving at Eaton a few days before the gardens were due to be open, having flown over in the private plane, he discovered there was an unexplained package with his luggage. It was addressed to the Duke, but he could not account for it, having ordered nothing special to be put aboard for transporting to Eaton. On being opened, this parcel was found to contain a large number of plastic blooms – daffodils, of course! In the parcel was a note in Major Hamilton Stubber's writing saying "Will these solve the problem?"

Before the war, the days the gardens were open provided a day out for many of the people not only from Chester, but from many miles around and even from as far afield as Liverpool, Manchester and the cotton towns of Lancashire. Many trips were organised to bring the visitors to Eaton by road, by rail and up the river Dee. The steamer trips left the Groves in Chester and disembarked their passengers at the "iron bridge". This bridge, a cast-iron one built in 1824, carries a drive over the river between Aldford and the Hall, and left the garden visitors a most pleasant walk alongside a lake and through the park before visiting the gardens.

The gardeners were always on duty on these open days to answer any questions that visitors may ask, and also to ensure that no blooms or cuttings were surreptitiously put into handbags or pockets. Children could and sometimes did run riot when let loose in these delightful surroundings, but the presence of the garden staff ensured no great damage was done.

The garden openings provided a welcome income for a number of charities, mostly Chester branches of national organisations such as the Red Cross, but should it turn out to be a day of inclement weather the attendance could be very low and this led to a perhaps unjustified feeling of unfairness: one charity would have a goodly sum for its funds and another would not do so well. However, Robert, the fifth Duke, realised this and after agreeing to various charities receiving benefits from the opening of the gardens, laid down that the season's taking should be shared amongst the charities concerned, a most sensible way to resolve that little bit of ill feeling.

The iron bridge has been mentioned as the point of disembarkation for steamer passengers from Chester. They really were steamers at one time, being propelled by steam-driven engines, but today they are mainly diesel-engined boats. At the iron bridge, a Jimmy Probyn was the proprietor of a café where afternoon tea could be taken. There also a rowing boat or two could be hired, and many people travelled from Chester to hire a boat for a pleasant trip up the less crowded reaches of the river. Tea could be taken at any time from eleven in the morning until well into the evening throughout the summer months, and for many years this must have been a thriving business. The Farndon strawberry and cream teas were known far and wide, and on a lovely sunny Sunday, the lawns between the house and the river would be crowded with people enjoying the food and scenery.

Today, unfortunately, no longer do the steamers *Flying Fox*, *Ormonde* and *Bend-Or* unload their passengers on the landing stage at the iron bridge, no longer are strawberry teas available or boats to hire at this delightful spot. Motor cars have changed peoples' habits, but perhaps one day the sheer volume of traffic on the roads will send people back to the pleasure of a cruise up the river.

The large numbers of people afoot in the park and on the river at Eaton demanded attention to security. Before 1939 the drives had never been barred to pedestrians or cyclists, and many local people enjoyed a walk of a summer's evening, particularly when the drive-side bushes of rhodendrons were a blaze of colour. Another favourite spot was Primrose Hill; early in the spring this place would be one mass of yellow, and the plants multiplied over the years to such an extent that they covered an acre or two. Patches of wonderfully scented violets could be found, the garden variety which must have been planted in a bygone era, and later in the year many of the drive-side verges abounded with wild strawberries.

With all this bounty of nature it was rare for anyone to take advantage and gather bunches of the blooms, although the fact that one of the large number of gamekeepers working on the estate was liable to appear at any moment must have been a great deterrent. There was really only one stipulation about taking a walk along these colourful and attractive drives, and that was no dogs – most definitely no dogs, not even on a lead. Should anyone attempt to take a dog in the park and be caught, they were barred to all intents and purposes from entering the estate again. The reason for this was that game abounded and any dogs, particularly any running wild, would create havoc amongst the pheasants.

Fifty years ago, security was part of the job for the game-keepers, especially those whose beats were adjacent to the hall. As long as people were walking the drives and kept moving, little notice was taken of them, but people even

77

walking on the grass were kept under close observation and nearly always warned to keep to the drive. From May to September a member of the Cheshire police force was hired to keep an eye on the visiting public and, touring the drives on his cycle, was a prominent part of the summer scene. He would work a normal eight-hour day, but the hours were put in at his own discretion or as occasion demanded, which made for a high degree of security. It's pretty certain that those bobbies loved being seconded to work at Eaton for the summer months.

After the second world war, and after the death of Bend-Or in 1953, the number of gamekeepers employed was very small, the park had changed in character and many of the drives had also lost their attractive appearance. Few people walked through the park, preferring to travel on four wheels, and these changes demanded a different approach to security. Estate employees and members of the golf club receive a car pass, while a certain number of people can also pay for the privilege of driving through the park, but they are usually vetted to prevent any undesirable folk having access to the grounds. To ensure that the conditions of issue of these passes are observed, there is a round-the-clock, round-the-year security staff. These men, who include an ex-police officer and one of the gamekeepers transferred to this department, are also responsible for security at the Hall and have to maintain a ceaseless vigil, using all the modern aids of security.

The gamekeepers and other key personnel are all equipped with personal radios. Many times the gamekeepers have been very grateful for this means of informing the security man on duty of the presence of poachers or any other undesirable activity. At the same time, the security staff know that they can call for help from the game department should help be needed. These modern aids of communication have to be a great boon, for the poacher of earlier years was a very different character from his modern counterpart. Today, transport plays a large part in his activities, and he often travels a great distance by car or van to pursue his nefarious ways. It makes the gamekeeper's job that more difficult — in fact, but for the radio contact available, almost impossible. The old-time poacher, on the other hand, was often a fairly local man, and went about his business either on foot or by cycle.

Many years ago, one dark and windy night in November, I was patrolling my beat when I came across two bikes partly hidden in a dense hedge. It was pretty obvious that poachers were about and, as it was a good night for the job, almost certainly rabbit-netting. Being on my own, I decided to contact one of my colleagues, but of course I had no pocket radio in those days. On reaching the highway I flagged down a car which, by sheer chance, was being driven by the policeman from Waverton, a nearby village. Alf Woodcock, the policeman, was naturally interested when I told him about the hidden bikes and agreed to wait and see whether the owners returned, hopefully loaded with rabbits and tackle.

After waiting an hour or more, Alf said, "I'm due off duty at 2 am and it's one past now."

"What shall we do?" asks I.

"Well, I reckon we'll take those bikes to your house and I'll report them as found abandoned," replies Alf. "Fair enough," says I. "If we don't find the owners, we might win a couple of bikes."

On arriving at my house, Alf was naturally asked if he would like a cup of tea. "Aye, not a bad idea," says Alf, "as long as the bottom half is whisky." The beverage was duly produced, and sandwiches to go with it, and eventually Alf set sail for his home at after four o'clock that morning.

The next morning the policeman from Farndon, a village just off Eaton Estate on the Welsh side, called on me and informed me that he had two chaps coming from Wrexham later that day, who had reported their bikes being stolen. Alf had obviously put word round his colleagues. After being given all the facts, the Farndon policeman said, "We'll learn those customers a lesson." They were going to come on the bus to Farndon, where he would meet them and then make them walk to Aldford, a distance of three miles, to collect their bikes. He wouldn't bring them to my house, but make them wait on the main road, "while we have a cup of tea and make out the necessary documents," he said.

Late that afternoon the Farndon bobby arrived at my

house with a grin on his face. "Do you know what tale they tell about last night? They reckon they'd been mushrooming." Fancy mushrooming in November on a pitch black night! It transpired that they had had to walk home to Wrexham the previous night, some ten miles, and then a further three miles to get their bikes back the next day. That particular pair were not known to come to Eaton again after rabbits.

Pheasants are a particular attraction to a certain class of poacher, and one such character started visiting Eaton Woods. He usually came late on a Sunday afternoon, often shooting a couple of birds as soon as they had gone up to roost. Naturally, the keepers soon became aware of these activities and laid plans to deal with the miscreant. It was decided that all eight keepers should meet at a farm roughly at the centre of the area the poacher had been in the habit of visiting practically every Sunday for a month. They were to arrive soon after lunch and as unobtrusively as possible. It meant a long wait, but keepers are used to that – as a rule they are very patient men

Late that afternoon a shot was heard and by chance it was in the wood closest to the farm. The pre-arranged plan was then put into operation: six of the keepers were to surround the wood, while the other two would enter the wood, one from each end, and flush the poacher out.

Walking slowly up the wood, and keeping a sharp eye out for any signs of the intruder, I suddenly came upon the poacher pushing his way through some blackberry bushes. As I saw him, a hen pheasant rose, and the poacher lifted his

gun and fired, killing the bird. By sheer chance, I had a large oak to hide behind as the pellets rattled all round me, and a good job too – a charge of pellets from a shotgun at twenty yards or so can inflict a lot of damage. As soon as the poacher made to pick up the shot pheasant, I shouted, and the man disentangled himself from the briars and took to his heels, only to run straight into a keeper waiting at the edge of the wood. He was fined the maximum possible for those days, ten pounds, and had his gun confiscated. He was another poacher we never saw again at Eaton!

6

When is a village a village, and not a hamlet? Many country folk would say that without a church and a public house, it can only be a hamlet, but there are places in between, some with a church and no pub, and then there can be a church right out in the country, between two hamlets. All this is the pattern of the English rural life; maybe the church has been left out on its own when the population has moved.

Before the second world war, the civil administration of these country districts such as the villages on Eaton Estate was the responsibility of a rural district council which would often have a vast area to care for. Councillors would be elected and represent a large number of parishes, but often a councillor was hardly known in many of the places he represented, which was not really a satisfactory arrangement. In 1949 it was decided that all areas should have a parish council, and at last the smaller villages could have some say in civil affairs.

Naturally these councils were elected by democratic means, through the ballot box, and this created some interesting incidents. At Aldford, where eight councillors were to be elected, there were almost twenty candidates, half of them ladies of the village. Yet not one lady got onto the council, and even with the passage of time, Aldford Parish Council still consists of all men. What's more, the pattern is identical in the next village of Saighton. All the same, the first Aldford Parish Council represented a fair cross-section of village life: an accountant, a couple of farmers, the grounds-man of Eaton Golf Course, a shepherd, the schoolmaster and a gamekeeper. Percy Smith, an accountant, was elected the first Chairman of Aldford Parish Council, and held this post for a number of years. Some of the early meetings were at least entertaining, although there was often a lot of talk about trivial things and many times no action was taken.

On one occasion, John Thomas, the schoolmaster, brought up the matter of a warning notice for the river Dee. It appeared that he had been taking the older children from the school down to the river to swim at a spot called Churton sand beds, and although at that point the water was shallow, it fell off sharply into deep water with a swift undertow current. One child had got into this deep water and had been in some danger of drowning, so John Thomas had had to dive into the water fully clothed. A notice-board was essential according to John, as it had become the custom for some children to go and swim without an adult in attendance on a warm summer evening. The council appreciated this danger but one of the farmers pointed out that generations of children had learnt to swim there without any disaster. John Thomas was not impressed and insisted that the council take some action, which he duly proposed. This was seconded, but as the Chairman was putting it to the vote, Tom Broster said, "Eh, boss, ain't them there sand beds in another parish? They ain't in Aldford." A map was produced, and it was discovered that the place in question was indeed about two hundred yards over the parish boundary! At that time the village of Churton had no council and Farndon was the nearest, so John Thomas insisted that the clerk write to Farndon, with a request for a notice to be erected at the sand beds. Nothing has been done, thirty years later!

John Thomas, being the schoolmaster, always had plenty to say at council meetings. He also had a habit, when the Chairman called for any other business, of jumping to his feet and saying, "It has just occurred to me, Mr Chairman." He would then bring something up that had already been dealt with. Percy Smith, the Chairman, was a patient man and put up with this for a good many meetings. Eventually, enough was enough and instead of calling for any other business, he said, "If nothing has just occurred to Mr Thomas, I declare the meeting closed." There was no more trouble from the vociferous schoolteacher.

The public rarely take much interest in parish council affairs, but one subject that crops up at regular intervals is street lights. Now the parish of Aldford covers a large area and the houses are well spaced out, so the village has over a mile of road. Each time this matter has been brought up the council have rejected it on the grounds of cost, but also because of the change it would make to such a lovely village. Aldford has remained virtually unchanged this century, people are used to getting around in the dark, and certainly the older people would hate to see the character of such sur-roundings spoilt by what would in effect be another step towards urbanisation.

Since that first council was formed over thirty years ago there have been many changes in its format. Most of the original council members are no longer on this earth, one or two have resigned and in fact I am the only member of the original council still serving, now as Chairman. Aldford Parish Council is now Aldford, Saighton and District Council, which takes in several small parishes, one with only three or four houses! One thing that the council is greatly interested in is the various planning applications which now have to come before them for comment and approval. This is a great step forward from the old days, and ensures that nothing unsightly is erected to spoil the delights of this area of the Cheshire countryside.

Otherwise it is mostly mundane things that appear on the

council agenda, but overall a village council does give a service to the inhabitants which would undoubtedly be missed. The councillors are unpaid and normally non-political, but all have a sense of responsibility to the electorate and most of all a desire to keep the countryside as it should be, a pleasure for people to travel through, visit or live in. May there always be real countrymen ready to serve their villages.

Living conditions in the villages served by such councils have improved greatly over the last fifty years. Very few cottages are as they were then, most have been modernised, and in Cheshire the Eaton Estate in particular has done a vast amount of work to improve the lot of its tenants. Fifty years ago, though, life was hard for the housewife. The husband usually had to start work pretty early in the morning, which made a long day for the wife. It was rare for her man to come home for a midday meal, so "snapping" (an old Cheshire word for sandwiches) had to be cut for his midday break. This was often prepared the night before, but with none of the modern packing materials available it was not always in the most edible condition on a hot summer day! For a drink at lunchtime there were no Thermos flasks in those days, so the farmworkers were often provided with a jug of tea from the farmhouse, but some who worked for less charitable farmers would take a bottle of cold milkless tea with them – not very warming on a cold winter's day!

The estate workers, particularly the woodmen, used a billy-can and brewed their tea in the woods. This was usually the job of the youngest member of the gang, the "can lad". Woe betide this lad if the tea was "stewed" or tasted of smoke, and it was not always easy to avoid this when he had to deal with maybe a dozen billies. Lighting the fire was an art in itself, but the old hands made sure the lad could do this job – they weren't going to be tea-less at "bagging time"! Even lighting a fire properly is a dying art, but those old boys could get a fire going on a pouring wet day without the use of paper. There was always something available to use as kindling. One favourite was slivers of bark from the silver birch tree, another the dead twigs of an elder bush, but no matter what they used, it wasn't long before the first glimmer of flame was built up to a roaring fire. Should the foresters have brush to burn, a separate fire was always made by the can lad, usually in a sheltered spot, where the men would congregate at the midday break.

The household washing was a major operation when the old-fashioned wash boiler was the only means available. In many cases the boiler was situated in a separate building, often a lean-to on the cottage. It held about fifteen gallons of water and so took a considerable while to get to the required temperature for the weekly wash. If the wind was in the wrong direction, those old boilers would smoke like the devil, which was not conducive to ideal washing conditions. Nevertheless, the housewives somehow managed what, by today's standards, was often a huge wash. It was not at all unusual for there to be anything up to a dozen children in each family, and how the devil they managed to exist in those mostly three-bedroomed cottages is indeed a mystery, let alone how the poor wife managed to do the weekly wash under such primitive conditions.

Of course, after the washing came the ironing, and none of your thermostatically controlled irons then, just the old cast smoothing-iron which had to be heated on the open fire and cleaned before use, and this repeated at frequent intervals. Even with two or three irons in the fire it was a laborious task, yet the results were remarkable. Some of the girls' frilly Sunday dresses were a real picture – much more attractive than today's sloppy and deliberately patched jeans!

Hot water for any purpose had to be heated on the old-fashioned range, which itself had to be black-leaded almost every morning, a somewhat daunting task for the modern housewife. Bath-night must have been a nightmare, for with a large number of grubby children to deal with, even with two in a slipper bath at a time, the water would be on the cool side before all had been soaked.

All housework was much harder in those so-called good old days. Floor coverings were few and far between; maybe the odd room was lino-covered but it was rare indeed to find a cottage with a stair carpet. Wooden stairs needed scrubbing now and again and the living rooms, with their tiled floors, needed daily attention. The local "Buckley" tile was rather coarse, which made it almost impossible to keep clean under normal conditions, while with numerous small feet tramping in and out, the task was made even more difficult. The door-steps were nearly always red raddled, and often the corner-stones of any out-building, such was the pride of those hard-worked housewives.

Oil lamps were the only means of lighting, a few of which are still around today, but the countryman of those days rose early, often before dawn, so bedtime was in most cases no later than ten pm. Around 1930, electricity was brought to Aldford and the neighbouring village of Churton, and that was when the great changes in domestic country life really began. Gradually all the dwellings were wired for power, the farms first, but what a godsend to the hard-pressed house-wife. Electric kettles were the priority, then came electric irons and not long after, in a case of keeping up with the Joneses, electric cookers. The lighting of the cottages was also much appreciated. One old lady, a widow, took a lot of per-suading to have "that new-fangled thing" installed, but eventually succumbed. The electrician duly arrived and pro-ceeded to do the necessary wiring, but later that evening the widow, greatly flustered, arrived at the local policeman's house. Seeing how agitated she was, he wondered what could have happened, but he eventually extracted from her the cause of her great concern. She wanted the bobby to come round to her house and to plug up the holes before the elec-tricity all escaped. She was of course referring to the holes in the socket which the electrician had installed for her to plug a kettle or iron into! It was a long while before the policeman could convince her that there would be no wastage and even-tually, no doubt, she was well pleased with the new source of power.

Before electricity was brought to the rural areas, radios, or wireless sets as they were called then, were not in every household. Each set was powered by a couple of accumu-lators, not batteries as today, and it was then a weekly chore to take one of the accumulators to be charged and bring back a charged one. This meant at one time a trip into Chester, five miles from Aldford, usually undertaken on a pushbike! It cost threepence for the charging of the accumulator, not much by today's prices but no doubt an item to be considered out of a wage of thirty-six shillings a week.

The Eaton Estate always looked after its employees well, and still does. It was the custom to provide enough material to decorate one room per year. This was standard for all cottages, but although all rooms in every cottage looked the same, the occupants were grateful. Lime was used for the ceilings, duck-egg blue for the top half of the walls, with a chocolate brown for the bottom half – this dark colour showing the dirt less, it must be assumed! This tended to make for very dreary rooms. Imagine what it was like on a winter's night with only the glow from a log fire and an oil lamp for illumination. Even under those conditions the housewife had the sewing, darning, and knitting to do.

Now that most rural cottages have been completely modernised, certainly on the Eaton Estate, living conditions compare very favourably with urban areas. With all mod cons installed and a car in the garage, life in the rural areas is much more pleasant than in those bygone days, yet people still seem to have little time to spare. They call it a rat-race today, but aren't too many folk really chasing shadows? Tom Broster, that old character affectionately called "The Cornerstone", said something when describing a certain lady that can be applied to many people, if only loosely. He said, "She rarely knows what she wants, and when she's got it, she doesn't know what to do with it!"

This is true of a lot of people who now live in country areas. They come from the towns and think everything will be wonderful, but it's only wonderful if you work to make it so. Only then can you appreciate the wonders of nature. A cottage garden doesn't just happen: much loving care is needed, and not just for an hour or two during spring weekends but all the year round. Concrete paths and gnomes under the front window are artificial and only an easy way out, but so many cottages in the rural areas are just that today, and it is a certain bet that the occupants come from a long line of city-dwellers. The old countryman knows all the easy ways of keeping a cottage garden in spick and span condition, but rarely indeed does he stoop to garish ornamental plastic urns, plastic gnomes and the like. They are not for him. The good old-fashioned flowers are much more attractive and in the long run probably less labour. What is nicer than a bed of sweet williams in full bloom, or a border of common asters in all its many colours during August? No expensive greenhouses or heat are required for these countrymen's favourites, nor for many other easy-to-grow plants.

Vegetables are an important part of a village garden, more so in bygone days than now; with often eight or ten mouths to feed, the more that could be grown the better. Most gardens in rural cottages were and in some cases still are quite large, anything up to half an acre. Most of this land was given over to producing as many vegetables as possible, but usually sticking to the most productive crops and things that would keep well through the often hard winters. The front garden, nevertheless, always had a good show of flowers in spring and summer, and there was often a border of blooms to the vegetable plot.

Many even quite small villages used to hold vegetable and flower shows which created friendly rivalry, particularly in the open classes. The show was usually followed by a dance on the lawn, with the music supplied by a brass band from the area, and what enjoyable nights those were, with fairy lights glimmering in the trees and the courting couples disappearing into the shadows as the night wore on! Would it be the same with a modern disco providing the music in such a sylvan setting?

The open classes at such shows could be entered by villagers from the surrounding areas, usually in a given radius of the particular show, and in the end were probably the cause of these enjoyable small shows coming to an end. Friendly rivalry was all right, but it got beyond that stage and some of the competitors would go to any lengths to win the prizes, despite the fact that these were really only nominal – half a crown, or maybe five shillings. Sometimes even that was in the form of vouchers, to be spent at local seed shops.

It was not unusual for some of those competing in the open classes to go to any lengths to get hold of a prize-winning specimen of, say, cauliflower, runner bean or onion. With a large area of the Dee valley being given over to market gardening, there was a plentiful supply of most vegetables to

choose from, and the unscrupulous entrants in these shows would often go to this area and, with the co-operation of the growers, have the choice of any particular crop. This attitude was not at all popular with the local village people and caused bickering and ill-feeling. Some even thought that the exhibits by the locals looked like "imported" veg.

One exhibitor, a genuine, dedicated cottager who took part in these shows many years ago continued to grow for exhibition all his life and won literally hundreds of prizes all over the country, particularly at the famous Southport Show. This was Walter ("Watty") Huxley, the forester mentioned in Chapter 1 for his hedge-laying skill and a real countryman by any standard. During the summer his garden was a veritable Aladdin's cave of vegetables. No matter what Watty decided to grow, he could somehow grow it better than anybody else: runner beans thirty-seven and a half inches long, giant onions that would sit on a bucket and broad beans and peas with more seed to the pod than anyone else's. In the *Guinness Book of Records* for growing the largest runner bean in a countryside competition, and winner of several cups outright, with medals galore, Watty was in his element when competing, not only with garden produce and in hedge-laying but in other fields as well.

A great athlete in his youth, Watty won many short-distance races but specialised in the long jump. There is a tributary of the river Dee that meanders through the village of Aldford, and on boggy ground beside this brook are the withen beds already described. Watty was involved in harvesting the withens and, being a man of a humorous character, would on occasions persuade the younger withen-cutters to try to jump the brook. This brook is near to twenty feet wide and to show it was quite possible, Watty would take a long run and leap the stretch of water with room to spare – no mean feat in working boots and with rough ground as a take-off point. The youths, often not knowing Watty's reputation and ability, naturally thought that if he could do it, so could they! After a tremendous run and a good take-off, the inevitable happened and they always landed in the brook! These pranks took place when the water wouldn't be very warm, withens having to be cut when the sap is down.

But back to those small village shows which are no longer
a part of rural Cheshire life — a loss to the community as a
whole and the villagers in particular. No longer is there the
incentive to try and beat your neighbour with your efforts in
the garden, and even the housewife misses out, since she no
longer makes cakes and jam to enter in the competitions at
the village flower and vegetable show. With a flower show in
the village there was a reason to grow everything as well as
possible, even amongst the less interested villagers, for there
was always the chance that something might do extra well and
be worth entering at the annual event, to make it possible to
pull the leg of more dedicated growers. Today there are still
one or two men who take part in shows up and down the
country but by and large the majority seem to look for the
easy way to do the gardening. The younger folk in particular
seem to favour rotivating the garden instead of digging it,
and fertilisers and sprays take the place of farmyard manure
and the scuffle, or hoe. This does at least keep the gardens
reasonably tidy, but somehow the crops do not seem quite the
same, and as far as vegetables are concerned, the use of fertilisers has altered the taste.

Other factors have changed the appearance of gardens in
the villages. In the old days, when a widow had a large
garden there were always relatives and friends to keep it in
order, mainly because they also lived in the village. Today,
even sons have moved to city and suburban areas, often some
distance away. Because of this greater movement of the
younger working people, widows are often left with few
friends, and even those can be as incapable as themselves.
This, plus the fact that some of the younger people know that
their stay in a village is going to be short and so do little in
the garden, tends to reduce the overall appearance, for only a
couple of gardens left to go rough can spoil the attraction of a
row of otherwise reasonably well-kept gardens.

This difference has been particularly marked over the last
ten to fifteen years. Soon after the Best-Kept Village competition was started in Cheshire about twenty years ago,
Aldford won the section for villages of its size and that was a
night to be remembered! Colonel Gerald Grosvenor, later to
become the fourth Duke of Westminster, gave instructions

that all drinks in the village pub, the Grosvenor Arms, were to be free. The pub was usually well supported by the villagers, but that evening it was literally crowded!

In following years, Aldford came very close to winning again but did not succeed in doing so. Saighton, a neighbouring village, did get the award on one occasion, but as the years went by, the standards maintained in the gardens deteriorated, and since 1979 the parish councils have deemed it usless to enter this Best-Kept Village competition. A pity really, but with little interest shown by the residents, there is no support for this worthwhile competition.

For a number of years a Best-Kept Garden competition took place in the village of Aldford, for a cup presented by Anne, Duchess of Westminster. For a while interest was maintained but unfortunately, when the judges did their tour of the village, they found it was just a matter of choosing between four or five gardens out of a total of fifty or so. This competition came to an end when one cottager won the cup outright by coming first, three years in succession. Once again, lack of interest brought a very worthwhile event to a close.

Fortunately, the property on these Eaton Estate villages is well maintained. It gets a regular coat of paint and attention to minor faults, which does help to give a good appearance to the village. All estate houses are painted the same colour, and this gives a uniform look which in the country seems much better than some of the brilliant, nay, gaudy colours used in urban areas. With owner-occupiers it's a matter of choice, but a country village certainly blends in with its surroundings better than the urban "patchwork quilt" effect.

One tradition on these estate villages which has fortunately been maintained is the cutting of garden hedges. Most villages used to have an annual summer event, the "Wakes", and it was the custom to have all the garden hedges cut for this get-together of the rural community. It is rather remarkable that the newcomers to these villages do get their hedges cut by the appropriate date, even when they know little about the old-time Wakes.

These midsummer junketings started many generations ago, but today have almost disappeared and are no longer looked forward to as in the past. They used to be the high-light of the summer and took place between haymaking and corn harvest. Each village had its set date, in the case of Aldford the first Saturday after the first Sunday in July. Churton was the last Saturday in July, and so on. Some villages did not have these Wakes but had a Rushbearing Sunday. This was a religious festival, but was always preceded by a "do" on the Saturday.

Of all the villages on the Eaton Estate, Aldford probably had the most popular Wakes. This was because the events were organised by the Ancient Order of Oddfellows, Lord Belgrave Lodge and a large number of estate employees were members of this Lodge. The Oddfellows were a most important part of village life in those days, meeting as they did a great need by giving sickness benefit and help to the needy long before the days of the Welfare State and the National Health Service.

On Wakes day there would be much activity in the village. Most people expected relatives and friends to call on them before the day was out, so the work had to be finished before lunchtime. The celebrations being of a partly religious nature, it had become the custom to tidy up the graves in the churchyard. It was not at all unusual to see a dozen people in the churchyard any evening during the preceding week, all busy scrubbing the gravestones. Then on the Friday evening and Saturday morning, fresh flowers would appear on the graves, making a really colourful scene.

The day itself started with a parade of most of the members of the Oddfellows round the village, led by a local brass band, either the one from nearby Farndon, or from Churton. During the nineteen-thirties it was usually the Churton Coronation Band under Walter Huxley, bandmaster – that remarkable character once again showing his many talents! Those not actually taking part in the parade would be following up behind or, in the case of elderly people, be at their gates watching the procession pass. After a tour of the village there would be a short service at the church and then the large number of children who were junior members of the Oddfellows adjourned to the Grosvenor Arms where all were served with tea. The village would be alive with people

93

and a large crowd would gather on the school field to watch the children taking part in the sports which followed the tea. How the children managed to run and jump after a huge tea will always remain a mystery! There was always a fair amount of rivalry at these sports. Many of the children came from adjoining villages, so it was almost a village against village event, but with Aldford having numerous children, they usually came out overall winners.

There certainly were a lot of children in those days. One road in Aldford, less than a quarter of a mile long, is even today known by the older residents as "Kid Street", for at one time in the nineteen-thirties there were eighty-seven children in that one street, all under the age of fourteen which was school-leaving age! The Rector of the parish at that time, the Rev. Paddy Austin, on seeing the local nurse's cycle outside a house, inquired of a passer by whether Mrs So-and-so was ill. On being told she was giving birth to a child, he remarked, "For sure, now, that's a healthy complaint." A good many had healthy complaints along Kid Street in those days!

When the children's sports were over, most of the folk wended their way back to the Grosvenor Arms. On the pub lawn, Watty Huxley and the Coronation Band were now playing for dancing and although the lawn was quite a large one, it was always crowded. The rough surface of the lawn was not ideal for good dancing, but that did not prevent the lads and lasses from enjoying themelves. With frequent visits inside the hostelry, the scene soon became a merry one. In those days it was most unusual to see ladies within the doors of an inn, but of course, the lads had no hesitation in bringing drinks out to the girls, and as the light faded, many a lass had her first taste of alcohol in the shadows. Romance blossomed under those conditions, when the parents loosened the rein on their offspring. The festivities went on until almost midnight, the one night of the year when it was possible to get a drink after ten o'clock at night, but an extension in the licence until eleven-thirty meant many a thick head on the Sunday morning.

There was also a fun fair in attendance at these summer events. Simons' travelling fair would arrive in the village on the Thursday or Friday before the Wakes and set up its stalls and side shows on the field opposite the Grosvenor Arms. Its arrival was eagerly looked forward to by the children of the village, who would go almost into Chester to meet the steam engine drawing the vehicles laden with the brightly painted stalls and stands. There were roundabouts, hoop-la, swings, roll the penny, a rifle range, coconut shies, throw the darts and of course the ever-popular hobby horses. That was a question the children always asked a month or two before the Wakes: "Are the hobby horses coming this year?"

Shortly before the war a new entertainment arrived, the "chair-o-planes" and this was looked upon in some awe by many of the older people who did not like the idea of being swung round over the crowds at ever-increasing speed. No fun fair was complete without the fair organ, and each year new tunes had to be introduced, which greatly pleased the populace. All these shows were run by a steam engine driving a generator, and the noise of the engine and generator running, combined with the smell of oil and steam, gave these fun fairs an aura of their own.

Being the main annual event in the village, the fair was always well patronised, even if all the patrons weren't too popular with the Simons family. On the rifle range, where clay pipes had to be broken with an air rifle, one gentleman was eventually banned! One of the gamekeepers from the estate couldn't resist trying his hand with the air guns, and once he got the hang of it broke clay pipe after clay pipe. It was threepence for five shots, and a small prize was given if five pipes were broken. After he had won five or six prizes, the stall-holder no longer made the

95

gamekeeper welcome and eventually gave him half a crown to stay away! Something similar happened at the coconut shies: the local blacksmith, being well-built and strong as an ox, rarely failed to knock a coconut off every time he had a go, often smashing the nut and then insisting on a sound one from the proprietor! However, he was not banned from having a go, for as soon as he approached the stall, a crowd would gather to watch his prowess. The stall-holder, being like most of the fair folk rather persuasive, encouraged the onlookers to have a go, and this more than offset his losses from the accurate throwing of the blacksmith.

For a few years after the war of 1939–45 the fair still came to the Wakes, but as time went on interest in the annual event waned, not only at Aldford but in surrounding villages as well. Simons' fair had a round of events, moving from village to village, but as one event after another lost its support, it was no longer a viable business and this small family fun fair has not been heard of for some time. What a shame that these colourful country events have disappeared, probably never to return. The Wakes are still held at Aldford, but with fewer members in the local lodge of the Oddfellows it is but a shadow of earlier days, and how much longer it will carry on in its present form is anyone's guess. Now it is just a short service in the church, tea for the kids and a dance for the older folk. There is a fair chance that the event will die with the senior citizens who now try so hard to keep it going.

The next village to Aldford, Churton, had for generations a sports day the week after Aldford Wakes, but this too has gradually died out over the years. At one time it was a great rural event, with entrants to the open sports coming long distances. There was a great air of competition, which drew crowds from far and near. There was something for everyone, a fancy dress parade round the village led by the Coronation Band, adult sports, children's sports, at night dancing on the lawn of a large house, and of course all the fun of Simons' fair.

It was not at all unusual to see Watty Huxley conducting the band one minute and the next stripped off and taking part in his speciality, the long jump. What's more, for many years he was unbeatable! With advancing years Watty was quite naturally unable to compete, and after suffering a long illness had to give up most of his social activities. This eventually led to the dispersal of the band which he had worked so hard to build up and which was his pride and joy. He was a remarkable man; not only was he a self-taught musician, he also taught the village lads to play the brass instruments to such a high standard that the Coronation Band was in great demand over a very wide area. A few of those lads of Watty's training, now old men, have played in another band formed at Farndon, the next village to Churton, and they regularly play with the band in the Groves at Chester during the summer months.

Maybe if the Coronation Band had not been dispersed, the summer sports at Churton and Aldford Wakes might have maintained their interest, for a parade round a village without a band does not attract much attention, but really the lack of music is only part of it. Today people are so much more mobile that there are only a small number of truly rural folk in the villages. The younger generation seem to have no interest in their rural surroundings, preferring when they are old enough to get something with an engine, a motor cycle or car, and journey into the city for their entertainment – when they are not glued to that box of self-entertainment, the television set! Maybe one day the tide will turn and people will realise that self-made fun can give pleasure not only to those organising and taking part, but also to a larger number of people as well.

7

The second world war undoubtedly caused many changes in most country districts, and the estate villages at Eaton were no exception. Despite most villagers being employed in agriculture or forestry, quite a high proportion of men of military age were called to the colours. Encouraged by the second Duke of Westminster, as far back as the turn of the century many Eaton men had enrolled in the Cheshire Yeomanry, and they served their country in both world wars. In peacetime in those days few people had a holiday, but enlisting in the Yeomanry ensured a fortnight's training camp in the summer. This camp was often close to a seaside resort and was always looked forward to by these voluntary yeoman. For many it was a complete change from their day-to-day tasks, and a paid holiday at that. A week or two before the second world war broke out the Cheshire Yeomanry were mobilised, and this took away from home a number of estate men between the ages of eighteen and thirty. One such chap, Tom Broster, had just got married and, after a few weeks in camp in England, went overseas to the Middle East with his unit and did not see his wife for almost six years. As Tom often said after the war, though, at least he did come back whereas many more didn't.

In July 1940 the Local Defence Volunteers were formed and most of the remaining male staff had no option but to join. Sandy Myles, the head forester, was instructed to form the local unit. Having been an officer in the first world war, he had no hesitation in going round his staff of woodmen and just detailing them to be on duty at a certain time and at a certain place! He then duly appeared at those places and issued the assembled company with the later familiar arm-band marked "LDV".

Later an Observer Corps section was formed, mostly of the older residents (many of them first world war veterans), and kept a twenty-four-hour watch for hostile aircraft. It was a very exhausting time for those men, for many of them were still following their occupations, yet the post was always manned.

These men, both full-time serving and volunteers, brought quite a change to the villages, particularly Aldford, when the war was over and they all returned to their civilian occupations. The comradeship and dependence on their fellow-men gave most a different outlook on life, and often made them restless and uneasy, unable to settle down to the same routine as before the war. There was a spirit afoot of wanting to do something. Several of the returned ex-service-men joined the Special Constables and gave further, this time practically unpaid, service to their country.

There had been in Aldford since 1926 an Ex-Servicemen's Association. No-one knows why it wasn't formed until that date, but it appears that several of the local farmers suddenly decided that they would like to do something for the first world war veterans and arranged a dinner in the local hostelry. From that date the Association came into being, but during the 1939—45 hostilities it was in abeyance. Naturally the men who returned from the second do were keen to revive this Association and in 1948 the annual dinner was revived. This was a great get-together of what was in effect an exclusive club, albeit in a modest way. The rules of joining were definite and adhered to: a person had to have been born in the village, gone to school in the village or joined the forces from the village. Members of the LDV and Observer Corps and ladies were excluded, but even so the membership at one time was over a hundred! The annual dinner in those days usually had one or two guests, as much as anything to make a speech or two, and often the General from Western Command took his seat at the top table. The Association is still going today, but changes have had to be made and each member is allowed to bring one guest, thus keeping the numbers attending to a respectable level. In 1981 there was still one first world war veteran at the dinner, a man in his eighty-fourth year with a record of not having missed a dinner since 1926!

There has always been entertainment provided at these functions, many of them excellent "turns", but of course there has always been some amusement from the members themselves. Tom Broster, a long-time chairman, usually rendered "The Blackbird", a favourite with servicemen, but with Tom's actions it was hilarious. He was a man of over twenty stones with a girth of fifty-nine inches, and when he was on the stage in his "funeral" suit and flapping his jacket like the wings of a bird, it was easy to imagine a blackbird! Another ditty he loved to perform was "Lloyd George knows my Father, Father knows Lloyd George" These were the only words and after a number of verses Tom would call for one more verse: "Come on, lads, let's have the thirty-second verse!" For some unknown reason it was always the thirty-second!

In the mid-nineteen-fifties, Colonel Gerald Grosvenor came to live on the Eaton Estate as head of the Grosvenor family following the death of the second Duke of Westminster in 1953. Although the second Duke had only attended the annual dinner on one occasion, he had always been Patron and had nearly always provided venison for the event. When Colonel Grosvenor arrived, it was only natural that he should be asked to become Patron of the Association; he was delighted and attended every annual dinner for many years. On his death, his brother, Lord Robert Grosvenor, became the fifth Duke of Westminster, and without being asked said he would like to be the Patron of the Assocation. The present young sixth Duke always attends the annual dinner as Patron, following the family tradition.

Things have changed quite a lot over the years: on the formation of the "Ex-Servicemen", the membership fee was one shilling and sixpence per quarter, and this pricely sum paid for the dinner, and benevolence for sick members, plus a barrel of beer which was consumed at the dinner. In the nineteen-fifties the fee was four shillings a year and dinner tickets three shillings. Benevolence was one pound if a member was off sick for fourteen days and two pounds a quarter for long-term sick members, but as time went by it became more difficult to keep this up. What had been the only money-raising event, a whist drive, did not bring in enough money to help the needy members, so several ideas were tried, including a sponsored fishing match for children. The Duke was delighted to give permission for it to take place on safe private water in Eaton Park, the Serpentine.

Other events were still needed to help the Assocation, and after exploring many avenues several members formed a party called the "Rosebuds and Stooges", the Rosebuds being for the most part ex-servicemen's wives. This gang put on sketches in the village hall. The sketches being written by local lads with a local theme, they filled the hall. With an auction sale of donated items afterwards, they raised quite a bit of money. Today in a village like Alford, benevolence is no longer a need, so the Ex-Servicemen's Association has not quite the same function and, with the passage of time, there is not the same spirit abroad, although the annual dinner still takes place in November.

As the sketches put on by the Rosebuds and Stooges needed very little in the way of scenery or props, many trips were made to villages in the area to entertain the people there. Of course, some research on the village to be visited had to be done, so that names of local people and places could be introduced into the scripts. These introductions aways caused a lot of amusement, but there was never anything to embarrass people – on the contrary, they were usually pleased to be mentioned.

On one such expedition to a village called Burwardsley,

pronounced "Bosley" in Cheshire, the usual arrangements had been made – half the profits to Burwardsley and half to Aldford. Now after these shows had been put on it was always the custom to entertain the visiting party before they left for home. This particular evening things had gone very well, the hall had been packed with an appreciative audience and everyone was in high spirits, which meant it was rather late before the Stooges got back home to Aldford. Nevertheless Albert Thomas, the treasurer, decided that the chairman and secretary, who were travelling in Albert's car, should call and have a nightcap. When the drinks were poured out, Albert thought the cash may as well be checked while the chairman and secretary were there. The total tallied with the figure given at Burwardsley so all was well, but then Albert decided to get the necessary bags to put the numerous small coins in. The kitchen table was covered with the old-fashioned tablecloth with matted tassels all around, and as

Albert jumped up one of his jacket buttons got entangled in the tassels and he pulled the cloth with him, scattering the coins all over the kitchen floor. The coins rolled in all directions, some under the huge Welsh dresser, some under the large sofa, and all around the kitchen range. Just imagine three men on their hands and knees, one of them over twenty stones, hunting those coins on a floor of very old, uneven, brown and grey mottled Buckley tiles in a huge old farmhouse kitchen, with the only illumination one forty-watt electric light! After some considerable time no more coins were to be found, but on the total being checked once again, this time without the tablecloth on, it was found to be one halfpenny short! To this day the Stooges' balance sheet still shows this discrepancy, a deliberate and amusing reminder of the incident.

The Wakes have been mentioned earlier, but to introduce something different one year, the Stooges committee decided to hold a comical tug-o'-war across Aldford brook. About forty feet wide where it is spanned by the main Chester Road bridge, this brook on the edge of the village made an ideal site for such a test of strength. Charlie Leyfield, formerly a trainer at Everton Football Club, appeared as umpire, in a two-seater canoe under the control of a local farmer, Nye

Pickering. Things went tremendously well, and of course the losing team landed up in the brook, to the great amusement of the huge crowd. In the end the winning team also jumped into the four-foot-deep water and overturned the canoe, umpire and all, to the shrieks of laughter of the spectators. This became an annual event for a number of years and received quite a lot of publicity from the press and television. A collection would be taken and the proceeds shared between the church and chapel. As the years went by, so many teams began to enter that eliminating pulls had to take place on dry land earlier in the week, but in the end "needle" began to creep in and many teams would turn up without fancy dress, so reluctantly the event was dropped from the Stooges' calendar.

The Rosebuds and Stooges were by no means a unique organisation, but the capers which they got up to were part of the rural life on Eaton Estate. All the events were to raise money either for good causes or for the celebration of a national event. Thus 1953, the Coronation Year of Queen Elizabeth II, was a great year for the Rosebuds and Stooges. Under the chairmanship of Tom Broster, many events were organised to ensure that there was enough money to make it a right Royal occasion in the village. Early in the spring of that year, it was decided to have a comic Ladies' Football Match, and in order to create more interest and make more money, the next village of Churton was drawn into the plan. The match was played between the villages on the school field at Aldford, in front of a large crowd. Charlie Leyfield was the referee once again, and the local lads were all at hand in various guises to add humour to the proceedings. Tom Broster was in full regalia as "Mayor of Aldford", wearing an old-fashioned frock coat, striped trousers and top hat and with a string of horse brasses as the mayoral chain. The Mayoress was another of the Stooges, Fred Thomas, who took the part perfectly with a large hat over a flowing wig, a discreet dress, stockings, high-heeled shoes and plenty of make-up.

At the end of the match, which the Rosebuds won by seven goals to six, came the presentation of the prize. Of course it had to be a cup, but the way the Stooges worked, it had to be

an unusual one. After a short speech by the "Mayor", the cup was presented to the captain of the Rosebuds team, Doris Powley. When she held it aloft, it was seen to be a willow-pattern chamber-pot well decked out in red, white and blue ribbon! Howls of laughter from the spectators, which must have been heard at Churton a mile and a half away. The event was a great success and added a considerable sum of money to the celebration funds of both Aldford and Churton.

Throughout the early months of 1953, fund-raising went on apace and a committee was set up to co-ordinate the celebrations. The main event was to be the roasting of a whole ox donated by Nye Pickering, but many foods were still rationed in 1953, including meat, so application had to be made to the Ministry of Food for permission to kill and roast the ox. The first application was turned down because permission could only be given to "bodies of people who have made a custom of roasting oxen at Coronations" and there was no record of oxen being roasted at Aldford during the present century! Enquiries were made through certain channels and an appeal against the decision sent off. Just three weeks before the great day, permission to roast was received from the Ministry of Food Head Office, but time was getting short. Ox-roasting entails a lot of work and quite a bit of equipment.

There was nobody in Aldford with knowledge of roasting a whole ox, so the only chance was a visit to Tilston, to see the man who had done the job in that village for many years. Harry Brereton was his name, a proper rural character and a man hard to pin down. The first visit was non-productive: he was not the slightest bit interested and would not even give any information on the job, but the gang sent to negotiate with him returned laden with garden produce, having spent the morning inspecting his large and excellent garden! They did discover that he always went to the local hostelry, the Wet Lanes, at Sunday lunchtime. A foray was planned to buttonhole him in the pub the following Sunday and try to persuade him, by the use of copious jars of "tonsil varnish", to come to Aldford and roast the ox on Coronation Day.

Tom Broster was the leader of the party, a persuasive man, and this time determined not to take "no" for an answer! Harry was in the pub when the party arrived, and straightaway said, "I know what you lot want, but nay, I'll have a pint!" Harry's glass was always full that lunchtime, but when the time came to leave, ox-roasting had not been mentioned. Tom guided Harry to his bike – he needed a bit of guiding by now – and as he tried to mount the cycle, Tom said, "We'll come and see you next Sunday, Harry. You can have a fiver in advance to roast that ox." Harry was quite indignant, parked his bike against the wall, staggered over to Tom and said, "I've never taken money for roasting an ox yet, and I ain't going to start, but I'll be down at Oddford tomorrow evening 'bout seven."

Sure enough he was, and described exactly what was wanted. The process of roasting would take at least twenty hours, and with two men on duty with Harry in two-hour spells, eighteen volunteers were needed. The process would go on throughout the night, and it was no easy task to persuade men to take a turn on duty, say from two to four am.

For a week before Coronation Day there was much activity on the pub field, where the roasing was to take place. The local blacksmith, "Tiny" Broster (Tom's cousin, and a man of six feet three inches!) had made an excellent job of the spit, which consisted of a spindle passed more or less centrally through the carcass and resting on two strong brackets either side of the fire. Beneath the ox was a large sheet of metal acting as a drip tray, and surrounding this a brick wall was built on three sides to throw the heat back onto the meat.

A day or two before the roasting was to take place, Nye Pickering arranged for a butcher to kill and dress the beast he was so generously giving to the festivities in the village. It was in prime condition, with a lot more meat on it than the villagers could eat on their own. No matter – many people would come from surrounding villages and even from Chester itself, and all would be welcome.

Harry Brereton was the only person who knew anything about this type of cooking so he fixed the time at which the fire should be lighted. He said that the roasting should be completed about three hours before the first slice was cut and, after inspecting the carcass before it was put on the spit,

105

decided that eight o'clock in the evening of 1st June would be about the right time to get the fire going.

It was a heavy, humid evening, after a hot day or two, with not a breath of air to fan the flames, so there was smoke everywhere. One wit remarked, "I've had smoked bacon, smoked herrings, and even tasted smoked salmon, but I ain't going to reckon much of smoked beef!" Eventually the fire got going, and within the hour it was throwing out a good heat and melting the dripping which had been spread liberally over the joint. Fat to spread over the carcass had been a problem, being still on ration, but local butchers had turned up trumps and although not really enough was available, Harry was certain that the beast was carrying enough fat to offset this shortage once the fire generated enough heat.

Thus the long vigil began, stoking, turning the spit and basting with the fat which soon began to accumulate in the bucket at the end of the drip tray. Once all was going well, "Harry the roaster" wended his way across the road to the Grosvenor Arms for a pint of well-earned ale. He was made very welcome, and during his whole visit to the village never had to put his hand in his pocket. On his return to the site he inspected the carcass, pronounced eveything to be satisfactory and adjourned to the tent which had been put up for him, with instructions to be called if the flesh became black or started to burn.

Harry wasn't to get much rest. A terrific thunderstorm broke out in the early hours of the morning and the men on duty were fearful that the fire would be doused by the torrential rain. No fear of the flesh burning – just the opposite! Harry had to be roused, and of course he wasn't too amused, being in a deep sleep after several pints of ale the evening before. "Throw some more wood on, and those few lumps of coal, get it backed up with coke and don't let the damned thing go out," he instructed. Harry and his two helpers worked frantically in the pouring rain and managed to keep a reasonable fire going, but with such a downpour all the fat had been washed off the carcass and the drip bucket was full of a mixture of water and grease. Once the fire was going nicely again, frantic basting had to be done, and as the downpour eased amid clouds of steam from the watered fat, the position improved and Harry was able to return to his slumbers.

Those slumbers must have been rather restless because, although Tom Broster had promised Harry a country breakfast, he did not anticipate the hour that he would be calling for it. At five-thirty on the morning of 2nd June there came a loud ram-tam on Tom's door. Poking his head through the bedroom window, Tom was rather surprised to see Harry at the door, and was greeted with "Come on down, you idle b———. I'm hungry. Where's that breakfast?" Mrs Broster had to be roused and it wasn't long before the three were sitting down to a breakfast of bacon, eggs, sausage, mushrooms and fried bread, washed down with copious cups of hot tea.

Fortunately the storm in the night had cleared, and all was going well with the roasting of the ox. During the day bread rolls had to be collected from Chester and tables and tools laid out for the ceremony of cutting the first slice, bunting had to be hung from poles and the tent decorated, until the site took on a carnival atmosphere. Someone remembered that beef needed mustard, and a lad was dispatched to the village Post Office-cum-shop to buy up its entire stock of the condiment. It was mixed in pound jam-jars, so there was an adequate supply available when the time came to eat the tasty meat.

During the afternoon, the children had sports on the school field, followed by a scrumptious tea and a fancy-dress parade. Meanwhile, most of the ladies were busily engaged in the parish hall preparing food for the evening's events. An electrical shop in the nearby village of Holt had very kindly installed a television set in the room where they were preparing the food. It was a black and white set, of course, but many of the women hadn't ever seen television before and no doubt the presence of the set contributed to the numbers helping to make the sandwiches, trifles, jellies and numerous trimmings. At one stage I popped in to see how things were going. When I came out, I reported, "The amount of grub there looks very promising, but have you ever seen about twenty women round three tables? It's confusion, but I hope it's organised confusion!" It was organised all right, as we

107

discovered when the time came to deal with what was a mountain of food.

At eight o'clock that evening the time had arrived to find out the result of so much labour on the ox-roasting field. Several local men had been appointed to assist in the carving, from a woodman, adept at carving sticks, to a chap who worked in a fish shop in Chester and was used to filleting fish. These men were under the supervision of Nye Pickering's butcher friend, just to make sure all would go well. Nye himself, as donor of the beast, had been invited to cut the first slice. Right on time he appeared out of the tent, dressed for the part in white jacket, white apron, chef's hat and brandishing a huge carving knife. Soon the carvers got to work and despite the size of the beast, very little was left after an hour or so.

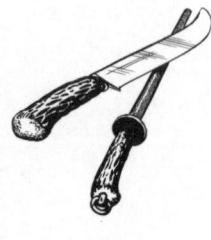

Later in the parish hall, the band played almost non-stop until the early hours, many of the dances being performed over and over again. When the pub closed the hall was bursting at the seams, but with everyone in a festive mood there were no problems, and of course the day ended with the National Anthem. Why isn't it played at more events today?

An ox is still roasted most years at the Cheshire village of Tilston, and Harry Brereton the ox-roaster is usually there, but these days in an advisory capacity. How long before another old rural activity is a thing of the past? Yes, barbecues do take place, but what has a "bag of mystery" (sausage) got to compare with a slice of well-roasted beef?

There was not even a thought of such an ambitious event as roasting an ox twenty-five years later, for Queen Elizabeth's Silver Jubilee in 1977. A public meeting was called in Aldford with celebrations in mind, but there were few ideas about money-raising functions. Gone were the days of ladies' football matches, a tug-o'-war across the brook and the like. Bingo was suggested, and a house-to-house collection, and that was the sum total of money-raising ventures. A house-to-house collection, yes, but in the old days there was always something to go with it – a gang of Stooges dressed up as gipsies, or a race of some sort round the village. "Give 'em something, even if it's nowt, and they'll give generously": that was Tom Broster's philosophy and it certainly worked. It was even decided at a parish council meeting that spring to give five pounds to the Jubilee Celebrations fund. I told the council in no uncertain terms that if it was necessary to beg a grant from the council, there must be something wrong with the Jubilee organising committee! Five pounds was only a little over one penny per inhabitant of the village, and a fat lot of difference that would make to any celebrations. However, these days any addition to the fund is gratefully received, as long as no working for it is involved.

The day of the Jubilee itself went off well, with the usual sports, tea and fancy-dress parade for the children, then later in the evening a social-cum-dance in the village hall for the older residents. But somehow there wasn't the fun of building up to the event, as in the old days. The money was raised so easily and with so little effort that the day itself was not appreciated as much as it could have been. Maybe the reason was that so few people were involved in raising money and organising the day.

Similarly, on the occasion of the marriage of Prince Charles and Lady Diana Spencer in 1981, there was little interest in having a "do" for all in the village of Aldford. In the end it was decided to celebrate the occasion, but with just a fancy-dress parade and tea for the children, followed later by a dance and social for the adults. A muted disco provided the music, but it seemed rather artificial music compared with the four-piece band of the old days. It did not pass unnoticed that eleven years earlier, in fact the day after Prince Charles' twenty-first birthday, he had been at a lunch in that very hall whilst spending a day shooting with the Duke of Westminster.

So Royal occasions have always been times of celebration in the country, and before the days of radio and television any excuse was pounced on to have a "do". With the changes taking place in all walks of life there seems much less interest in rural events of this nature, yet the countryman who cares to can remember how much fun was to be had at little cost when events were being held to raise funds for a big celebration in the community that was his village.

8

Estates in rural areas mean villages and hamlets, and fifty years ago these pockets of habitation were lively, vibrant places. Any area of population had its own church and very often a chapel as well, and even quite small hamlets would have their own school, where the person responsible for their spiritual needs would take a service at least once a month. Nearly every service had a large congregation – what a difference to these days of poor attendances, even allowing for smaller numbers of people working on the land. Men and women working on the land in any shape or form, in fact anyone working close to nature, seem to have a deeper sense of religion than many other people. Country folk are in a position to observe all the wonders of nature and to appreciate the changes from winter to spring to summer and then to harvest in the autumn. This closeness to the land has its effect, and although the churches may be sparsely attended at most times, Harvest Festival still nearly always sees a good country church full.

In an earlier age, the squire or landlord of a large estate went a long way towards keeping the finances of these country churches in a healthy state, and in many cases the churches were built or rebuilt by these benevolent people. The livings of these churches sometimes had advantages that went with them. One instance is the church at Bangor-on-Dee, some twelve miles or so from Eaton Estate. For many years the Grosvenor family, possibly back to the Marquess of Grosvenor in the last century, had the living of the parish church at Bangor, and with it went a one-mile stretch of river fishing. This water was about the nearest stretch of rod fishing for salmon: the Dee still carries a lot of salmon, but there is little doubt that fewer now pass the weir at Chester on their way upstream to spawn. Another link between the church and salmon: netting salmon has taken place for a century or two below the weir in Chester, and right back to bygone days it has always been the custom to present the lucky rector of the nearest church, St Mary's Without the Walls, with the first salmon caught when the season starts.

111

Today, with less salmon being netted, it is normal practice for the first fish caught to be taken and shown to the rector, who then claims a prime cut for his own use and the fisherman sells the remainder.

The days of tithes have long since gone, but in the village of Aldford there still remains a large, well-maintained building between the church and the house that used to be the rectory. This building was where tithes had to be paid and, judging by the size of the building in relation to the size of the village, the dues must have been pretty heavy.

Many rural churches had a large house as the rectory or vicarage. The reverend gentlemen then must have been much better off than their modern counterparts, for it would cost a fortune just to heat some of their houses during the winter months. Wood must have played a big part in the heating of these buildings and no doubt those situated on an estate like Eaton would get a generous allowance free. It needed at least one and sometimes two servants to do the housework, plus a man to keep the grounds in good order. It is pretty obvious that a lot of the vicars in those days must have had private means and did not rely entirely on their stipend. One such parson, Paddy Austin of Aldford, kept a horse to ride around his rather scattered parish and was also fond of hunting. He always arranged it that if the hounds were meeting close by, he had some visiting to do in the area they were likely to come to. He would tie his horse outside a cottage and spend a lot of time ministering to, perhaps, an aged pensioner, but at the slightest sign of the hounds approaching he would be through the door, up on his horse and away to join in the hunt. That was the last of his visiting the sick and aged that day; he would follow the hounds until they finished for the day, and sometimes he could be seen hacking his way home on a very tired horse as dusk fell. Truly a hunting parson, but not at all unusual fifty years ago!

In due fairness to the Rev. Paddy Austin, he did spend a lot of time visiting his flock, but he had the knack of arriving around meal times, no doubt with a cup of tea and a piece of cake in mind, which was not too popular with a lot of people. Local policemen had the same knack! On one occasion, Paddy called at a farmhouse just at tea time. The

112

farmer's wife had been a bit pestered by a lot of visitors that week, and had had no time to bake a fresh supply of cakes. Paddy opened the back door and walked into the kitchen, as was the custom of the reverend gentlemen in those days. The table was laid for tea and the son of the household, a lad of about seven years, was sitting by the fire. The farmer's wife was caught unawares when Paddy walked in but soon pulled herself together, saying, "Do you want a bite to eat, vicar?"

Paddy replied, "I would be most grateful for a little sustenance to see me on my way. God bless you, my dear."

The farmer's wife said, "Well, I don't know what I can find for you", and straightaway the little lad by the fire shouted, "Give the old b——— an egg, mum."

Paddy stopped for his tea, but it was some time before he visited that particular farm at meal time again.

With all cottages having large gardens, it was not at all unusual to see the womenfolk working outside during the summer months, and Paddy was in his element when he could catch a lady working thus. He would always stride up the garden path and offer his help with whatever the lady was doing. He seemed to specialise in helping to thin onions – he must have been very fond of them because he would often take a bunch of the thinned onions away with him, enough to satisfy a dozen people. Perhaps the man was wrongly judged, and he took the spring onions to older people who were without, but in any case as far as the lady gardener was concerned, Paddy was very welcome to them, especially if he did the thinning himself.

The vicar's wife always played a great part in village activities. As today, she was the enrolling member for the Mothers' Union, and so had reason to visit a lot of the houses. Mrs Austin lived up to this idea of a vicar's wife and carried out her duties as fully as anyone could wish. She made a point of visiting any newly married young ladies who came to reside on her patch, maybe thinking of the future but mainly to enquire if they were happy and looking after their new husband. Unfortunately, Mrs Austin was not afraid of giving advice, some of it rather outspoken, and sometimes she would find the door locked, having been spotted before she had reached the house.

Parsons come and go but the churches remain, and long may they do so. One incumbent at Aldford, a single man, had no wish to occupy the large rectory, although his sister was going to keep house for him. When he first arrived there was not a suitable cottage in the village available, so until one became vacant the vicar took lodgings in the local pub, the Grosvenor Arms. This in itself was breaking away from tradition, but as one local wag told him, "You're in the right place if you want to do any converting, parson." He would occasionally join the locals for a half of ale in the bar, but also had the habit of standing at the top of the stairs, more or less out of sight, listening to the conversation. Naturally this did not go down well with the local tipplers, so one evening one of the lads shouted up to him, "Come on down, rector, thee'll hear a damn sight better, if thee's sitting with us."

"Cedric", as he had been nicknamed for no known reason, had little alternative but to join the gang and take his turn in buying a round!

Another vicar, of a parish not far from Aldford, was once caught poaching pheasants, trapping them actually. Not wishing to create too much furore over the incident, I quietly told the Duke, at that time Gerald, the fourth, about what had happened. His response was to say the least a little unexpected: "I'd rather have a parson that poached my pheasants than a parson who poached another man's wife!" It was never clear whether the Duke knew something that I didn't about the local clergy, or if he was referring to some incident in the past. In any case, no action was taken against the poaching parson – in fact, he received a brace of pheasants from the Duke at Christmas – but he ceased his poaching activities.

In those days the vicar seemed to have a lot of power and was respected, or even held in some awe, by the village people. Should a parson ask anyone why they weren't in church last Sunday, you could be sure they would be there the next. Being called upon to serve on the committees of almost all village organisations, frequently as chairman, also increased the vicar's influence over the populace. Rarely would a villager refuse to do what a parson asked, not even try to make excuses, so the rural parson held almost as much power and authority as the landlord or squire.

Eventually, mainly because of the fall in congregation numbers and the cost of having a vicar for every church, the smaller parishes lost a resident spiritual leader. Most vicars now have a large area in their care, sometimes with as many as three churches to preach in in one day. Nearly all rural parsons have two churches, which means that evensong takes place on alternate Sundays in each place of worship, and vice versa the morning service, an arrangement which seems to work quite well although some parishes still lament the loss of a resident parson.

What an even greater loss it would be if the day should come when there was no village church, especially for christenings, funerals and above all weddings. It was most unusual in the old days for a country girl to be wed other than in her own church, where she had more than likely been christened and quite probably sung in the choir. The celebrations after a village wedding were always lavish, but on a smaller scale than is seen today. The bride's home was always the venue, where a ham and chicken wedding breakfast would be held for relatives and friends. A big "do" with a barrel or two of ale was a good sign, for no matter how poor the parents, this was one occasion that had to have the full treatment. Should it be on a very small scale, it was considered that something was amiss, and so many times this was proved right. One old character had a saying about these frugal celebrations: "Aye, I dare bet they've tapped the barrel afore the Wakes." He meant that the bride in question was pregnant, a situation which naturally shamed the parents of those days.

Modern parents have different standards and no matter what the situation, a large "do" is called for. The reception is held either in the village hall, with caterers brought in for the meal, or in a local hotel which can cope with a hundred or more guests. It's got to be champagne now as opposed to a glass of sherry in the old days. Nine village weddings out of ten also have a dance or disco in the evening and more often than not the bride and bridegroom are there. Many have a honeymoon abroad – a trip along the coast to Rhyl or Blackpool for a few days is no use to the modern youth who can go that far any week-end in the car.

115

For many years there had been no Grosvenor family weddings, at least from Eaton. Bend-Or, although married several times, usually chose a registry office for the ceremony, but when Robert, the fifth Duke, took up residence with his two daughters and son, there was a family at Eaton. Eventually the daughters, Lady Leonora and Lady Jane, were married from Eaton. Lady Leonora married Patrick, Lord Lichfield, and this was a great occasion. The wedding took place at Chester Cathedral, and on that Saturday morning the town almost came to a standstill. A large number of the Royal Family were present, which naturally drew huge crowds. Everything had been arranged like a military operation. All guests, other than family, had to report to a car park in Chester, the Little Roodee, and here buses were running a shuttle service to the Cathedral. After the ceremony a convoy of these buses took all the guests to Eaton, where a huge marquee had been erected. Some fourteen hundred guests were entertained to a sumptuous wedding breakfast, and after the happy couple had left by helicopter, the buses returned the revellers to their cars on the Little Roodee. Everyone crowded the area in front of the Hall to witness the couple's departure, the ladies in their colourful but rather flimsy hats. As the rotor blades of the helicopter started to turn, many hands grabbed for their headgear, but when the craft lifted from the ground and Lord and Lady Lichfield could be seen waving from the cabin, the hands were released to wave back. Several of those treasured pieces of the milliner's art rose into the air as a final salute to the bride and bridegroom!

Shortly after this great event at Eaton, Lady Leonora's sister, Lade Jane, married the young Duke of Roxburgh amid similar festivities. Lady Jane was married in the church at Eccleston, which could not accommodate as many guests as the Cathedral in Chester, so after a family ceremony the reception was held at Eaton, where many friends and estate workers from both Eaton and Floors Castle, the Duke of Roxburgh's seat in Scotland, wished the couple a happy future.

Lord Gerald Grosvenor, as he was when he married Miss Natalie Phillips, naturally had to abide by custom and have the ceremony and reception at the bride's parents' home, Luton Hoo in Bedfordshire. Once again the Grosvenors maintained their reputation as caring landlords and several busloads of people travelled from Chester down the motorway to be at the reception. Tenants and employees alike appreciate these opportunities to join in the Grosvenor family celebrations, and lavish celebrations they are. When Lord Grosvenor came of age in 1972, the vast marquee was like something out of Caribbean Nights. All the employees on the estate were invited, and the supply of food and drink was never-ending, culminating in breakfast at five in the morning. Dancing to Joe Loss's band and being entertained by exotic limbo dancers made it a night never to be forgotten.

With these young Grosvenors at Eaton there were more activities than for many years, but as the weddings took place and life changed for the "Ladies", it gradually went back to quieter days. Unfortunately the fifth Duke had been a sick man for some time, and was unable to be present at his son's wedding at Luton Hoo. He did return to his home at Eley Lodge in Northern Ireland, but never fully recovered and after suffering over a long period, finally passed away.

Funerals always bring a fair number of folk to church, particularly if the person who has died is young or has been a local character. A funeral in the nineteen-twenties was very different from today. If the cortège had half a mile or less to travel, the coffin was carried shoulder-high by the bearers, who would usually be friends and colleagues of the deceased. Should the last journey be an appreciable distance, a farm lorry would be used with the coffin resting on a bed of straw. If possible, black horses would be used even if the lorry came from one farm and the horse or horses from another. The mourners usually walked behind the coffin and as they passed through the village on the way to the church, the cottagers would have their blinds drawn. It is seldom that this custom of drawing the blinds or curtains is followed today, nor is the custom of relatives of a deceased person wearing a black armband, often for several months. After the first world war, the Ex-Servicemen's Fund had a bier made for use at funerals. This was a rather clumsy piece of

117

equipment, very difficult to manoeuvre between the pews in the church, but no doubt saved a lot of aching shoulders. Having quite large wheels, it was very suitable for use from the house to the church.

Gerald, the fourth Duke of Westminster, was buried at Eccleston, as all the Grosvenor family have been, in the family section of the graveyard. After lying in state in the church, he was buried with full military honours as befitted a Colonel and a very military gentleman. Vigil was kept over the coffin by two employees doing an hourly guard, which enabled all employees on the estate to take part. The coffin was carried by six workers who had been taken into Chester and kitted out with identical suits at the most expensive tailors in the town. The day the visit was made to the tailors, the next visit was to the undertakers where a rehearsal of the bearers' duties took place. Next to Eccleston church, to make sure that everyone was familiar with the funeral procedures. Although it was really a family and private funeral, the church was full of relatives and friends. The floral tributes filled the churchyard, and came in all shapes and forms and from all over the British isles. One tribute from the game-keepers at Eaton was in the shape of a gun and a dog, picked out in brown and white flowers to represent a spaniel – the Duke had reared spaniels of that colour for many years. Many, many more people would have liked to have been in church, but as it would only accomodate a limited number, the service was relayed to the village hall which allowed several hundred more people to take part in a tribute to a well-loved Duke and one of this world's gentlemen.

Being right on the borders of Wales, the estate had quite lot of "chapel" people. Today very few of these places of worship on Eaton Estate are still in use, but at one time they would draw a large congregation. According to tales told by an old parisher, the children used to have quite a bit of fun at those chapel services. There was no resident preacher in the village, so parsons would come to take the Sunday services from either Chester or Wrexham. On one occasion when a passionate sermon was being delivered, a particularly religious member of the congregation kept shouting "Alleluia" and was soon joined by the others present, until a loud chorus resounded through the building. All of a sudden the leader of the chorus shouted in a loud voice, "I see him", followed by a silence and then a shout of "I've got him". Whereupon a squeaky voice from the back of the chapel was heard to say, "Well hold on to him, then we can all go home!" What a good hiding that child would get after the service!

After the second world war the attendance at these rural chapels declined and although a year or so ago a Harvest Festival service was held in the chapel at Aldford, it has now been sold for conversion into a residence – the passing of another era.

Eaton Hall has its own private chapel, which was used regularly when a large staff was employed, but today there are not many services held. The present Duke's two children have been christened there at private ceremonies. The Princess of Wales is godmother to the Duke and Duchess's second daughter, Edwina, and with the service taking place in the private chapel, it ensured a quiet week-end for the Princess, soon to become a mother herself. A memorial service for Robert, the fifth Duke, was held in this chapel, and was also private.

The livings of most of the churches on Eaton Estate were held by the Grosvenor family, and although Bend-Or, the second Duke, was not a great or regular churchgoer, his predecessors were and the Grosvenors that have followed him have been. It was part of the Sunday routine to attend church at either Eccleston or Aldford, the two nearest churches except for the chapel with its famous clock tower at Eaton itself. There is still a footpath from the Hall to Eccleston church. This path runs parallel with the drive, and although now overgrown in a number of places, it is a very attractive walk along a ridge of sandstone some height above the river Dee. It is very easy to conjure up a picture of the Grosvenor family taking a leisurely stroll on a Sunday morning in the spring. Passing through parkland and close to the river, no doubt a large variety of bird-song could be heard, and many wild spring flowers seen at their very best; there is no chance of absorbing these glories of spring if you flash by in the modern motor car.

The footpath to Aldford church was probably even more

attractive than the one to Eccleston, passing for a good distance through the grounds of the Hall and then crossing the river via the iron bridge before going across some fields to the church. The path across the fields was a made-up one, and in the old days would be edged, raked and cleaned every Saturday morning. On either side at intervals were planted groups of hawthorn trees, alternately white and a lovely pink. What a marvellous walk in the month of May! These paths were of course private and are still called the "Private Walks".

With the people from the "big house" attending one or other of the estate churches most Sundays, there was always a good congregation, no doubt much to the satisfaction of the clergy. The same thing does not apply today: Gerald, the sixth and present Duke, travels widely and is probably at home at Eaton on only five or six Sundays in the year. On these occasions he attends Eccleston church.

The church in rural areas has often taken a large responsibility for the education of the children of the parish. Many places in Cheshire still have schools which are linked to the church, but this link seems to be getting weaker. There are very few church-aided schools left, and the controlled ones seem to be closing down one after the other. Of course the number of children in the rural areas is declining as families become smaller and fewer people are actually working in the country, but there was a time when a village of less than two hundred people needed a school and that would be crowded. Now villages of five or six hundred population have not enough children to warrant keeping the school open. For example, at one time the village of Churton, half of which is on Eaton Estate, had its own school, and although the village had only about a hundred and fifty residents, the school needed two teachers. Closed many years ago, the school is now the village hall, but even so the church still keeps its link with the village and the rector from adjacent Aldford takes a monthly service there.

Aldford itself at one time had two Church schools, one for boys and one for girls. These were eventually amalgamated under one roof, and today Aldford school is about to be closed. It is a well-built establishment capable of taking three

120

classes in large classrooms, but only twelve children attend. Yet just over fifty years ago, the school was bursting at the seams, with over a hundred children busy learning the three "R's". Other schools on the estate have fared a little better, but mainly those close to the city. It would appear that many parents prefer their children to be educated in a rural school as opposed to an urban one, but only when transport is not a problem.

Will the children of the villagers suffer for this change in schools? Maybe they will get a slightly better education — though I wonder — but one thing is pretty certain: their interest in the countryside will be overwhelmed by the chatter and ideas of city children. It is very noticeable today that even the children who have had their primary education in a village school, and then moved on to an urban secondary or high school, lose interest in their village surroundings and want to go into the city whenever possible. Nature to these children no longer seems to be the fascinating thing it is. Biology lessons cannot compare with watching the changes of the seasons with interest and at first hand. The village schools had nature walks from an early age, and many interesting items were always on display in the classrooms. This, combined with the knowledge of their parents, meant that the children of yesteryear were well steeped in country lore. Maybe parents of today are so concerned about their children having qualifications, at least on paper, that there is little time to encourage love of the countryside. Maybe all these examinations, O-levels, A-levels and Higher Degrees, are absolutely essential for a school-leaver to obtain a job, but how much these children are missing cannot be calculated.

It is true that many more people are taking country walks, but do they really appreciate their surroundings when walking the rural footpaths? Even the fact that they are frequently dressed in brilliantly coloured anoraks and headgear indicates that they do not really appreciate the ways of the birds and animals. What's the use of field glasses when your dress is going to disturb and frighten so many of the natural inhabitants of field and wood?

Children of a generation or so ago could expect a good education in other ways from these village schools, and many

121

of them have done well in later life. One small village school has produced a secretary to a British Consul, now working in Mexico, a veterinary surgeon and several lads who have done exceptionally well in various police forces, reaching in at least one case the rank of Chief Inspector – not bad for children of country stock, educated mainly in rural surroundings.

9

Country churches have been discussed in the previous chapter, so now it is appropriate to turn to the country public house. In the old days the country pub was as different from the city hostelry as chalk is from cheese but today, mainly due to modern transport, the country pub with its juke box, one-armed bandit, Stars Wars machine and bar snacks draws many of its patrons from city and suburb. It is no longer the meeting-place of the workers on the land that it used to be; even they drive out of the village for their liquid refreshment.

Fifty years ago mild beer was four old pence a pint, and very few rural pubs sold bitter beer. Today, no matter where the public house is, there is a large variety of ales to choose from, none of them for less than ten bob in old money a pint! The different type of customer ensures the variety of beers, no doubt, but most old-timers were quite happy with their local brew, not some fancy and comparatively weak concoction, carted half the length of the country. It was only the better-off farmers who drank whisky. That was beyond the means of most country workers, who had maybe an odd nip for some special occasion, but the preference was for the cheaper ale, since three pints of ale lasted longer than one nip of whisky!

Women were never seen in the bars, but most licensed premises had a "jug and bottle" section. This was usually a very small place with a door to enter and a "pop hole" to serve the customer through. The local ladies would visit this section, present a jug and ask for "Just a pint for the old man's supper", when many times the "old man" would be in the bar, imbibing a pint! It was strange how those country women didn't want their neighbours to know that they enjoyed a glass of ale. The second world war changed all that, and now there can easily be as many women as men enjoying a night out, particularly at week-ends. It may be that there is no connection, but it certainly seems to have some bearing on the lack of rural characters in pubs these days. With the womenfolk present there is not the same "earthy" conversation that there used to be, and somehow in this restrained atmosphere rural humour has to a large degree disappeared.

Many landlords of pubs in rural areas did not rely entirely on the takings over the bar for their livelihood. Many had an acre or two of ground and kept a milking cow or two; most kept a pig and there were others who had full-time jobs. Today, most pubs are either owned or managed by large breweries, and the managers and tenants, although usually fond of the countryside, often have very little knowledge of it. Maybe it doesn't matter so much when most of their customers either travel out from urban areas or have moved out into the village and commute to work in the cities.

Many of the landlords were characters, too. This was good for business, no doubt, but what a cheerful place it made the country pub. One such man, Joe Lloyd, mine host at an inn in the heart of Cheshire, always took an interest in the people in the parish. He was an expert at basket-making with the local withens and whenever he heard that a local girl was getting married he would set to make her a wedding present. It was always the same – a baby's crib! This was really a masterpiece of the basket-maker's art, but many a young lady must have had mixed feelings when old Joe delivered it to her house. It was always accepted in the spirit in which it was given, though, and as a rule it came in very useful before a couple of years had passed!

The same Joe Lloyd did not take kindly to the progress of modern times. When it became fashionable for the youths to let their hair grow long, he would not entertain them at any price. Several who had been regular customers soon knew they were not welcome in the "Cat", the local name for Joe's pub, but one evening a couple of youths who were obviously not aware of Joe's attitude to the modern fashion entered the bar and asked for a couple of pints. Joe looked them up and down, saw the length of their hair and said, "Nay, lads, I wunny serve ye."

"Why not?" asked one of the youths.

"I'll tell ye why not" says Joe. "If ye canny afford a hair-cut, ye canny afford to sup my ale." And that was the end of the matter!

Other publicans took rather the same view of the modern youth. One such was Teddy Carlton, landlord of the Carden Arms in the village of Tilston. Teddy was a semi-retired producer of pantomimes, who really only took the pub for somewhere to live in lovely surroundings, and to give him the chance to talk to people. He was very fond of good humour and frequently had people from the world of entertainment stopping with him. Robb Wilton of monologue fame was a frequent guest, and it was said that much of the material that Robb used was gathered from the pub at Tilston. With Teddy behind the bar on a winter's night, with a huge log fire roaring away in the fireplace and Teddy's selected friends supping ale, it was a perfect example of a real old English tavern.

Teddy's friends were definitely selected; it was always said that if your face didn't fit, the Carden Arms was not a place where you were made welcome, and many of the villagers of Tilston seldom drank ale at the bar. Nevertheless, a trout fisherman who could talk with knowledge on the subject and tell a good tale was a welcome guest, while no-one with a fund of country lore was ever turned away. Less welcome

125

visitors were soon left in no doubt about Teddy's attitude, as on one occasion when two lads and two girls entered the bar carrying their crash-helmets. They appeared respectable enough, but Teddy cast a wary eye over them. One of the lads came to the bar and asked Teddy for the drinks he needed: "Two pints of bitter, a gin and tonic and a tomato juice, landlord."

The "landlord" bit irked Teddy somewhat – "mine host" he considered more appropriate – so he replied, "I can't serve you, lad."

"Why not?" was the reply. "We're all over eighteen."

"I don't care if you're over eighty" was Teddy's comment.

By now the youth was getting worked up, his companions had settled down by the fire and were waiting for drinks, so he raised his voice and said, "I demand to be served."

That did it. Teddy lifted the flap on the bar, came through and, with an outstretched arm pointing to the door, said in a calm but commanding voice, "That's the way out, and the door shuts from the other side." Exit four rather forlorn teenagers whose faces didn't fit!

The Carden Arms at one time had quite a good bowling green, but when Teddy took the pub over it fell into disuse, maybe because he did not take to the folk who had been playing there. One evening the green was brought up in discussion in the bar, and someone said they would like to roll a wood or two. "No problem," says Teddy, "I'll get it mown tomorrow. I've got some woods and we'll have a game."

The next day, as promised, Teddy got the local odd-job man to run the machine over what had once been the velvet turf of a bowling green but which had only been mown about twice a year for many years. That evening one or two regulars turned up with their sets of woods, knowing full well that the surface would be useless to bowl on, but at the same time wanting to humour Teddy. The "green" looked rather like the stubble on a cornfield. Still, some attempt had to be made, but after several bouncing deliveries of the woods, Teddy decided it "needs a shower to get the surface right." It needed more than that: a heavy roller, a shower and a few more mowings would have been a bit nearer the mark!

After that first evening little more was said about the game, but Teddy had the grass cut very regularly and a year or so later the game was brought up again by a couple of Teddy's regulars from Aldford. "Sure, lads," says Teddy. "There's some woods in the garage, have a go." There was no doubt the old lad was delighted, and he told each customer as they came in, "A game of bowls is in progress."

The lads came from Aldford a couple of times a week after that and had a bit of fun chasing the woods back and to across the lawn, for it was still far from being a bowling green. But as the weeks went by and the evenings drew in there was hardly time to get the woods out of the garage before the light had gone. One evening the "Aldford gang" walked into the bar and said, "We can't play tonight, it's too dark, Teddy."

"To dark be damned," says the old lad. "Come with me."

They all trooped out of the pub. Straight to the garage goes Teddy, backs the car out, swings it round and switches the headlights on. "You can see now, can't you," he says and goes back to serving beer.

There was no option but to get the woods out and have a go. Soon Teddy was out with pints of beer for the players

and bringing customers to watch the floodlit game of bowls. Each week after that it was the same, until there were too many worm-casts on the grass and it was too cold out of doors. When there was a heavy dew and the headlights shone through the spray thrown up by the woods, the rainbow caused was an unusual sight!

Such a man was Teddy that the floodlit players were never allowed to pay for any beer that he brought out to the green, so what with the beer and the wear on his car battery it must have been an expensive fad! In fact, the way Teddy Carlton ran that particular pub it is very doubtful if he ever made any money, but as all his old customers agreed, it was as a country pub should be – a place for company, good conversation, a bit of humour and fun, and last but not least a good pint of ale.

Each pub has its own atmosphere, but without doubt it was much more marked fifty years ago than it is today. With the sameness it is not easy to find any character like those who used to frequent the pubs. One such was "Ham" Mellor, a man of many parts who made a bob here and a bob there, turning his hand to practically any job that cropped up on the farms and not afraid of hard work. He was not often flush with money but somehow always managed to find his way to the pub with enough cash for a "latch-lifter", as he called it. By this he meant that he had a copper or two to open the pub door, and once inside with perhaps only half a pint of beer, hoped some kind soul would treat him to another drink. It was not unknown for him to walk the river bank on a Sunday evening looking for beer bottles discarded by the week-end fishermen; these he would take to the local pub, the White Horse in Churton, and claim the deposit of a penny a bottle. If he was lucky he would have enough pennies for a pint or two and be able to spend the evening by the bar.

Ham was also the gravedigger at the church at Coddington, a hamlet about three miles from Churton. He had done this job for many years, making his way to the distant churchyard on his old bike when a grave had to be dug. With the passing of years and the onset of the "screws", as he called rheumatism, it became more difficult not only to get to Coddington but to dig a grave. At last Ham decided the job was too much for him and he would have to resign from the post, so called on the parson to tell him of the position. Even though there were only two or three funerals a year in that remote hamlet, the parson was rather upset about the state of affairs, being at a loss to know where to get a replacement. He pleaded with Ham to carry on a bit longer, but to no avail: Ham's mind was made up. An offer of another shilling or so for each grave dug would not move him, but then the parson played what he thought was his trump card: he would bring him back and to in his car. Ham's face lit up and the parson thought, "Ah, that's done the trick." But Ham replied, "All right, then, sir, I'll carry on so long as you can guarantee me two graves a week." The parson was struck dumb and could think of no reply! No more graves were dug by the old lad but he eked out a living by various means and lived to a ripe old age.

Pubs always used to be the scene of friendly competitions, be it darts, dominoes or other unusual affairs like a moustache-growing competition. A number of years ago two workmates had a lively discussion about growing "face fungus", and in the end Ian Davies, a fair-haired chap, bet Tommy Green, an almost black-haired fellow, that he could grow a better moustache in six weeks than Tommy could. The bet was struck, and the loser was to buy the winner a bottle of whisky. It was all to be done in a fair and just way, with three judges being appointed, one for density, one for texture and one for overall appearance, each to award points out of ten. The judging was to take place in the "scratching shed", a bar in the Grosvenor Arms at Aldford, six weeks to the day hence.

The evening of the judging duly arrived and Ian was sure he would win. Tommy had been shaving until three weeks previously, but having dark hair gave him a great advantage, which Ian apparently hadn't realised when the bet was struck. When all were assembled in the "scratching shed", Ian, Tommy, the judges and spectators, it was very obvious that Ian had no chance. A fair assessment had to be made, however, and the judges made a great show of deciding what points should be awarded for their section. Tom Broster, who once again was taking part and was judging for density, produced

a huge magnifying-glass and examined the amount of growth at great length. When the points were added up, Tommy Green came out a handsome winner and Ian duly bought a bottle of whisky. It didn't take the assembled company long to dispose of the bottle, much to Tommy's dusgust!

Darts still play a part in most pubs, many having teams which travel from one hostelry to another, but years ago transport was not easily available so it was usually friendly events between the customers. Nevertheless, some away matches were played, the participants usually travelling on cycles. One such match had been arranged many years ago between the Grosvenor Arms at Aldford and the Plough at Isycoed, a village just over the Welsh border about five miles distant. The Plough was a really old pub, attached to a small farm, and naturally all the customers worked on the land in such a truly rural area of the Dee valley. The darts match was going well, with little difference between the skill of either side, and plenty of ale was being supped (no breathalyser in those days, and they were all on bikes or on foot anyway). The Plough was lit by oil lamps which were never very bright anyway, but as the evening wore on nobody noticed that the visibility was slowly getting worse. The last two were at the board, playing the deciding game of five hundred and one up, when it dawned on the Aldford player that it was pretty difficult to see the dart-board, let alone the numbers, and he remarked on the fact. Naturally all he got in reply were comments like "You've had too much ale", "Get your eyes tested" and "Don't make excuses".

In the by now very dim light, the Aldford player had little chance, being used to the brighter electric light at the Grosvenor, and the outcome was that the Plough lad won the game and the match for his side. Several Aldford players complained about the poor light, but the landlord said, "That lamp must be getting low on paraffin." As it was purely a social and friendly event no-one was really bothered, but later the Grosvenor team were convinced that some bright spark had surreptitiously turned the lamp down whenever the opportunity presented itself! Many years later, when a member of that darts team from Aldford called in at the by now modernised Plough, well lit and carpeted, an old lad from Isycoed mentioned that darts match of earlier days and freely admitted that it was the usual practice for the Plough team to dim the light if they looked like losing. The losing team always bought the winners a drink!

It must be remembered that a lot of the fun in rural lives usually centred around the nearest inn, so it was not uncommon to see the most unexpected things happening there. Fortunately, most of these things were done purely for the entertainment of those taking part and of the patrons not actually involved. The Black Dog at Waverton, a small Cheshire village on the edge of Eaton Estate, frequently had these friendly events. A butter-making competition seemed to crop up at intervals, when several butter churns would be on the forecourt and local worthies would see who could make a measured amount of cream into butter the fastest. There was a skill to this, but caution was thrown to the winds in the haste to turn the cream into butter – admittedly the quality of the finished product was not taken into account in judging the competition! This type of event pleased the landlord since it is thirsty work, turning a churn in a hurry.

Often at the same pub there would be friendly rivalry over producing the best, or rather largest, vegetables or fruit. The prize for the winner was a free pint. It was nearly always a Sunday lunchtime event, and according to the season, the local worthies would bring their produce to be judged by the landlord. He was no fool, for those competitions brought a lot of people to the pub who wouldn't normally be there of a Sunday lunchtime.

Today most inns have many young persons as customers, but years ago it was normally the older men who were the regular drinkers and a lad dared not put his nose through the door if his father was likely to be at the bar. This fraternity of older men must have been a factor in producing the many characters around, and many of them had their favourite sayings. Tom Broster was a man of many sayings, and on

131

entering a pub he would usually start off by saying, "Whose birthday is it today?" Of course it rarely was anybody's birthday, but that lack of a reason to celebrate didn't worry Tom one bit. If there was no response to his question, he would say, "Not to worry, I was born on Saint Swithun's day and I've been dry ever since." He was born on Saint Swithun's day, too!

Once, whilst talking to some strangers at the bar, Tom was asked where he lived. "At educational corner" was Tom's reply.

"Yes, but where's that?" came the question.

"Up the road by the rector," says Tom.'

"I see," said the stranger, "but why educational corner?"

"Well," says Tom, "the head schoolteacher lives next door to me, then comes the rector and I reckon to know a little bit myself!"

A man of ready wit was Tom. He was working one day on the golf course at Eaton when a stranger approached, whom Tom realised at once was a military gentleman. The stranger stopped and introduced himself: "I'm General Vyse of Western Command."

"Oh aye," says Tom, "and I'm Tom Broster of Aldford."

This undoubtedly pleased the General, for several years later, when he was guest speaker at an Ex-Servicemen's Association dinner at which Tom was chairman, Sir Howard Vyse brought into his speech how he came to meet Tom on the golf course.

Len Turney, another Eaton character, would always start any conversation with the comment, "As I was a-saying of to Annie", Annie being his wife. He would proceed to tell a tale that more than likely Annie had never heard of and possibly, in many cases, better that she hadn't! One night a chap came into the bar who had obviously been associated with some of Len's friends but did not know Len. This chap must have got into the habit of using Len's opening phrase for, after talking to Len for a while, he came out with "As I was a-saying of to Annie". There was a deadly hush and all eyes turned in their direction, but Len, obviously not wanting to create a commotion, said calmly, "Is your wife's name Annie too?" Of course it wasn't long before the

132

stranger was taken on one side by one of the regulars and the position explained to him. However, it was quite noticeable that Len Turney did not use the phrase about Annie quite so much after that.

Another old lad always said the same thing as he went through the door on his way home at closing time. It was really a very logical statement, but always caused some amusement to folks who might not have heard it before. It was simply: "Good night, all. If the Lord spares me, I'll keep coming here till I die."

At Aldford, hard by the Grosvenor Arms, are the village stocks. Little is known about this relic of the past, but they are even today in remarkably good condition. The wooden sections were renewed a number of years ago, it must be admitted, but this was the work of the Stooges, who had an ulterior motive in mind. At one of the many events held in the village, it was decided to "kidnap" the man who was running the hostelry at that time, John Lloyd (no relation to Joe Lloyd of the "Cat"). The object, of course, was a donation to the cause the Stooges were working for. All was set, and a number of the Stooges entered the pub quite casually. By some pretext they lured John through the main door, and as soon as he was outside he was hustled across the road into the stocks. Word soon got round, spread by the Stooges, and a fairly large crowd gathered. By now John's assistant had missed his boss and appeared on the scene. They are double-seated stocks so, without more ado and despite his protests, he found himself fastened by his ankles, too! John took it all in good part and soon calmed his assistant down but refused, with a twinkle in his eye, to give to the good cause. Tom Broster thought it might be a good idea to use a little persuasion, so, playing to the crowd, he sent one of his "minors" to the pub kitchen for a few tomatoes – "The softer the better," he said. These were handed out to the crowd and discharged in the direction of the helpless occupants of the stocks.

As soon as the supply of

tomatoes ran out, John Lloyd decided to capitulate, but before doing so he insisted that a collection be taken from the crowd present. A cigar tin was taken round the spectators and soon became quite heavy with the coins donated by generous persons who had witnessed what in the past was probably quite a common sight. It was three cheers for John and his companion, and then a rapid dash for the bar – it's surprising how thirsty laughter makes folk! John Lloyd was no fool; he didn't resist too much when the prank started, knowing full well that the Stooges always drew a crowd, and what better place than outside the Grosvenor Arms?

Pubs always seem to have a connection with those worthy members of the rural community, the village bobbies. Even the smallest country village had its local policeman before the war, and most of them were, in the right meaning of the word, countrymen. Although it was the practice in those days to move a policeman on every few years, it never took long for a new arrival to know all the inhabitants of his patch, particularly any villagers who at times were liable to stray from the straight and narrow path. There never was a lot of villainy in the villages – maybe the odd poacher, usually one who only took a rabbit for the pot, sometimes a farmworker who would return to the farm when he knew the farmer was out for the evening and "borrow" some feed for his pigs or poultry. The local bobby knew them all, and all about them, and when things went a bit too far, an odd word at the right time was usually enough fo put an end to such illegal activities.

The village children always viewed these men in blue with respect, not least because it was amazing what a flick on the ear with a pair of woollen gloves on a cold night could do! It didn't do the kids any harm, and there certainly wasn't the vandalism and disrespect from the young generation of fifty years ago that seems to prevail today. Even now, it must in fairness be said that children from rural areas are comparatively less trouble in this respect.

There were not the cars on the roads in the nineteen-thirties that there are today, but once children had cycles available they could travel around quite a bit and weren't too worried about a lamp on their cycle after dark. If they had one at all, it was either without paraffin or, if it was one of the old-fashioned carbide lamps, the carbide was flooded. If neither of these, then they had no way of lighting it because few parents allowed their offspring to carry matches around with them. One such lad was returning to Aldford from a visit to Saighton one autumn evening and, as so often happened, he had no light on his cycle. Getting close to home, he realised there was a light coming up behind him fast and put on speed, but no luck – he was overtaken by the policeman from Eccleston, another village on Eaton Estate. His name was taken in the proper manner and he was told he would be reported for riding without a light. In due course the case came up at Broxton Magistrates Court and the lad was fined half a crown. The ironic part was, the policeman was the lad's uncle!

A year or two after this incident, the same lad's father, who worked for the County Council, had been installing a "halt" sign at the bottom of a hill approaching Aldford, one of the first "halt" signs in the area. That night the old lad had to come down this road on his way home from the council depot and, as he had done so many times, came sailing gaily down the hill and straight past the newly erected sign without giving it a thought. Fifty yards further on he was stopped by a policeman, the same one who had stopped his son without a light, his own brother-in-law! It made no difference that he protested that he had helped erect the "halt" sign that very day. The only response he got was, "Well, if you don't know about it who will?" Fined ten shillings!

This just goes to show that despite living in an area and even having relatives there, those old village bobbies did their job without fear or favour. Maybe it might be as well to add that that particular policeman did retire with the rank of Sergeant!

Unlike his modern counterpart, the village policeman before the war did not have a radio, but with the changing times the village bobby has practically disappeared, being replaced by a mobile officer who has to cover a large area and can be directed anywhere by a call from his control room. It is a pity in some ways, but the only viable way for many of the smaller villages to have any police cover at all, in days

when even the smallest rural post office can so easily be raided by villains from many miles away.

Although many aspects of rural life, both past and present, have been covered in these chapters, many more have had to be left out. I hope, though, that enough have been described to demonstrate to the reader the change of character and change of characters in the part of Cheshire in which I have lived for the last half-century. Much of what I have written is inevitably nostalgic, and rightly so because so many good things have been lost from the countryside, but there are also encouraging signs of a great future for rural life.

The old style of country dweller has almost certainly gone forever, but the vast majority of English people have a great feeling for nature and the soil. Many things prove this – the popularity of nature programmes on television, the way urban and city people tend their often small gardens, and the number of bird-feeding tables and nesting boxes that can be seen. If the city dwellers who move out to the country to live will make friends of and listen to folk whose families have been country workers in one farm or another for several generations, all should be well in the future. When planning applications are put up for the approval of parish councils, let's hope every council has a true man of the soil among its members, and that other councillors, many of whom are very likely to be commuters, will heed any comments the villager may make.

A large part of south-west Cheshire is very fortunate in being comprised of fairly large estates and is in a very fortunate position because of this. Lord Tollemache at Peckforton, Major Barbour at Bolesworth, the Earl of Cholmondeley at Cholmondeley Castle, the trustees of Sir John Leech at Carden and the Duke of Westminster's Grosvenor Estates at Eaton are all very keen that the environment should be maintained and if possible improved, realising that it is so easy for so much to be lost, almost without being noticed, and that once it has gone it is almost impossible to bring back. Just one small proof of that: not all that many years ago, the corncrake was quite plentiful in the Cheshire countryside, and its rasping call could be heard almost anywhere any evening in the spring. Alas, it slowly dwindled until suddenly it no longer visited the lush spring countryside. It would be nice to hear it again!

Nevertheless, there does appear to be a general awakening to the dangers that man has been inflicting on the flora and fauna of our great English countryside. Past generations have cared and nurtured all that was good in this land of ours, and it is only right that each new generation should ensure that this heritage should be there for posterity. Everybody must play their part in seeing that there is no further deterioration. Nature on its own can do a lot – it will take care of extremes of weather such as severe frost or prolonged drought – but man can assist in so many ways if only by ensuring that no litter is left behind amongst the lanes and byways, by leaving the wild flowers to seed and multiply instead of gathering them to wilt and die in a vase at home, and by being as quiet as possible to avoid too much disturbance to our diminishing wildlife.

The author is like one of the two characters in a country pub who were each sitting with a pint-glass, half-full of ale. One said, "My jar's half-empty", to which the other replied,

"Mine's not, it's half-full." The first one then said, "Yours is the same as mine, half-empty", but he received the answer, "Ah, but there's a difference — you're a pessimist and I'm an optimist."

My pint-glass is half-full!

NORMAN MURSELL
ALDFORD, 1982